Number 114
Summer 2007

New Directions for Evaluation

Sandra Mathison
Editor-in-Chief

Enduring Issues in Evaluation: The 20th Anniversary of the Collaboration between NDE and AEA

Sandra Mathison
Editor

ENDURING ISSUES IN EVALUATION: The 20th Anniversary of the Collaboration between NDE and AEA
Sandra Mathison (ed.)
New Directions for Evaluation, no. 114
Sandra Mathison, Editor-in-Chief

Microfilm copies of issues and articles are available in 16mm and 35mm, as well as microfiche in 105mm, through University Microfilms Inc., 300 North Zeeb Road, Ann Arbor, Michigan 48106-1346.

New Directions for Evaluation is indexed in Cambridge Scientific Abstracts, Contents Pages in Education, Educational Research Abstracts Online, Higher Education Abstracts, Social Services Abstracts, Sociological Abstracts, and Worldwide Political Sciences Abstracts.

NEW DIRECTIONS FOR EVALUATION (ISSN 1097-6736, electronic ISSN 1534-875X) is part of The Jossey-Bass Education Series and is published quarterly by Wiley Subscription Services, Inc., A Wiley Company, at Jossey-Bass, 989 Market Street, San Francisco, California 94103-1741.

SUBSCRIPTIONS cost $80 for U.S./Canada/Mexico; $104 international. For institutions, agencies, and libraries, $199 U.S.; $239 Canada; $273 international. Prices subject to change.

EDITORIAL CORRESPONDENCE should be addressed to the Editor-in-Chief, Sandra Mathison, University of British Columbia, 2125 Main Mall, Vancouver, BC V6T 1Z4, Canada.

www.josseybass.com

June 29, 2007

Editorial Policy and Procedures

New Directions for Evaluation, a quarterly sourcebook, is an official publication of the American Evaluation Association. The journal publishes empirical, methodological, and theoretical works on all aspects of evaluation. A reflective approach to evaluation is an essential strand to be woven through every volume. The editors encourage volumes that have one of three foci: (1) craft volumes that present approaches, methods, or techniques that can be applied in evaluation practice, such as the use of templates, case studies, or survey research; (2) professional issue volumes that present issues of import for the field of evaluation, such as utilization of evaluation or locus of evaluation capacity; (3) societal issue volumes that draw out the implications of intellectual, social, or cultural developments for the field of evaluation, such as the women's movement, communitarianism, or multiculturalism. A wide range of substantive domains is appropriate for *New Directions for Evaluation;* however, the domains must be of interest to a large audience within the field of evaluation. We encourage a diversity of perspectives and experiences within each volume, as well as creative bridges between evaluation and other sectors of our collective lives.

The editors do not consider or publish unsolicited single manuscripts. Each issue of the journal is devoted to a single topic, with contributions solicited, organized, reviewed, and edited by a guest editor. Issues may take any of several forms, such as a series of related chapters, a debate, or a long article followed by brief critical commentaries. In all cases, the proposals must follow a specific format, which can be obtained from the editor-in-chief. These proposals are sent to members of the editorial board and to relevant substantive experts for peer review. The process may result in acceptance, a recommendation to revise and resubmit, or rejection. However, the editors are committed to working constructively with potential guest editors to help them develop acceptable proposals.

Sandra Mathison, Editor-in-Chief
University of British Columbia
2125 Main Mall
Vancouver, BC V6T 1Z4
CANADA
e-mail: nde@eval.org

CONTENTS

EDITOR'S NOTES

The American Evaluation Association (AEA) celebrated its twentieth birthday in 2006. The partnership between AEA and *New Directions for Evaluation* (NDE) has spanned this time, and indeed, stretches back further to AEA's predecessor associations, the Evaluation Research Society and ENet. This is the beginning of other celebrations as NDE's publishers approach important birthdays. This year Jossey-Bass is celebrating its fortieth anniversary, and John Wiley & Sons, which acquired Jossey-Bass in 1999, will celebrate its bicentennial year.

Anniversaries are memorable moments, key elements of history. They are backward glances, ones that make us think about high and low points, but also provide glimpses into a future, ones that extend past successes, remedy shortcomings, and blaze new pathways. Taking the opportunity to pause at anniversaries is an opportunity for edification.

This issue of *New Directions for Evaluation* looks back at the past twenty years, highlighting important moments and enduring issues in the discipline and profession of evaluation. The first chapter provides a brief analysis of the contents of NDE over the past twenty years and the simultaneous events occurring in the development and growth of the American Evaluation Association. Next, Lois-ellin Datta's chapter provides a very brief history of NDE, including the journal's purpose, the various foci, how the journal has operated, and such events as the change in the journal's name. But much of the issue is devoted to "greatest hits" chapters that have appeared in prior NDE issues. It was no small task to identify these chapters, but in the end, through consultation with the journal's editorial board and a careful analysis of citation indexes, four NDE chapters were selected. Each of the reprinted chapters is introduced by a preeminent evaluator's analysis of why that chapter has found a prominent place in the evaluation literature. You will notice that these chapters are about big ideas, ideas that have shaped and indeed will continue to shape how we think about and do evaluation. They deal with issues of validity, interpretation, causation, and the emergent importance of program theory and participatory approaches in evaluation. The issue concludes with a chapter by AEA's immediate past president, Mel Mark, who looks back on the development of the association and into the future by outlining new directions for AEA and the field of evaluation itself.

Although these four reprinted chapters have enjoyed very broad appeal, Daniel Stufflebeam's *Evaluation Models* issue tops the sales charts and certainly deserves a place on the "greatest hits" list—but space obviously

NEW DIRECTIONS FOR EVALUATION, no. 114, Summer 2007 © Wiley Periodicals, Inc.
Published online in Wiley InterScience (www.interscience.wiley.com) • DOI: 10.1002/ev.220

1

precludes reprinting a whole issue. The popularity of Stufflebeam's issue on evaluation models may indicate the field's desire for clarity about its models and methods. Stufflebeam provides a description and evaluation of twenty-two models of evaluation. Like this issue of NDE, Stufflebeam's analysis of evaluation models looks back at the value and utility of each model and then forward by identifying those with value, those with some promise, and those that perhaps ought to be abandoned. Whether readers agree or disagree with Stufflebeam's evaluative conclusions, clearly his treatise provides food for thought in formulations of evaluation theory and practice.

The reprinted chapters are presented in chronological order. The first greatest hit is Egon G. Guba and Yvonna S. Lincoln's 1986 chapter, "But Is It Rigorous? Trustworthiness and Authenticity in Naturalistic Evaluation," introduced by Thomas A. Schwandt. The second greatest hit is Mark Lipsey's 1993 chapter, "Theory as Method: Small Theories of Treatments," introduced by Laura C. Leviton. The third greatest hit is Carol Weiss's 1997 "Theory-Based Evaluation: Past, Present, and Future," introduced by Patricia J. Rogers. And the final greatest hit is C. Bradley Cousins and Elizabeth Whitmore's 1998 "Framing Participatory Evaluation," introduced by Jean A. King. The greatest hits chapters are followed by Anna Madison's analysis of the coverage of issues related to underrepresented groups over the past twenty years.

The past twenty years have seen continued growth in evaluation—the membership of AEA continues to rise each year, but paradoxically, formal university degree programs have diminished (Engle, Altschuld, and Kim, 2006), and external funding for evaluation has shrunk. The practice of evaluation seems, however, to remain strong. AEA plays an important role in the professional development of novice and expert evaluators through workshops at the annual meeting, and now a summer institute. NDE, along with other evaluation journals, also plays a significant role in sustaining dialogue about evaluation theory and practice: sharing analyses, stories, how-tos, and inviting deliberation. Twenty years into this partnership, it seems clear that AEA and NDE complement each other in their respective contributions to the evolving discipline of evaluation.

Sandra Mathison
Editor

Reference

Engle, M., Altschuld, J., and Kim, Y. "2002 Survey of Evaluation Preparation Programs in Universities." *American Journal of Evaluation*, 2006, 27(3), 353–359.

SANDRA MATHISON is professor of education at the University of British Columbia and editor-in-chief of New Directions for Evaluation.

NEW DIRECTIONS FOR EVALUATION • DOI: 10.1002/ev

1

This chapter introduces the celebration of the twentieth anniversary of the American Evaluation Association and its association with this journal, and offers an overview of important events and topics of discussion during the past two decades.

The Partnership of *New Directions for Evaluation* and the American Evaluation Association

Sandra Mathison

The American Evaluation Association (AEA) celebrated its twentieth birthday in 2006. The partnership between AEA and *New Directions for Evaluation* (NDE) has spanned this time, and indeed, stretches back further to AEA's precursor associations, the Evaluation Research Society and ENet. This is just the start of other celebrations as NDE's publishers approach important birthdays. This year Jossey-Bass is celebrating its fortieth anniversary and John Wiley & Sons, which acquired Jossey-Bass in 1999, will celebrate its bicentennial year.

Examining the contents of NDE over the past twenty years provides a window into evaluators' minds. The contents of NDE issues offer at least a partial picture of what evaluators have been thinking about and doing over the last two decades. A careful read of NDE volumes from 1986 through 2006 suggests the journal has primarily been a context for sharing methodological discussions, usually through a combination of description and case examples. Many of the issues are general discussions of evaluation methodology, and about a third focus on evaluation in particular contexts, such as human services, government, health, environment, or education. An equal number of issues have been devoted to qualitatively and quantitatively oriented methods, and two issues focused on the relationship between the two. More of the quantitatively focused issues were published in the first of these two decades, whereas more qualitatively focused issues appeared

NEW DIRECTIONS FOR EVALUATION, no. 114, Summer 2007   © Wiley Periodicals, Inc.
Published online in Wiley InterScience (www.interscience.wiley.com) • DOI: 10.1002/ev.221

3

Table 1.1. A Time Line of Important Events for the American Evaluation Association, 1986–2006

Year	President	Annual Conference Theme	NDE Editor-in-Chief	Notable Events
1986	Richard Light	*What Have We Learned*	Mark Lipsey	First annual meeting of AEA, the combined association of the former ENet and Evaluation Research Society.
1987	Robert Covert	*Utilization of Evaluation*		Long-range planning process for AEA initiated.
1988	Michael Patton	*Evaluation and Politics*		Merger agreement expired; AEA constitution and by-laws constituted.
1989	Ross F. Conner	*New Perspectives from International and Cross-Cultural Evaluation*	Nick Smith	San Francisco earthquake—annual meeting shortened to one day.
				AEA begins long-standing international commitment to evaluation development.
1990	Yvonna Lincoln	*Evaluation and the Formulation of Public Policy*		Height of the quantitative and qualitative debate in evaluation.
1991	Lee Sechrest	*New Evaluation Horizons*		
1992	David Cordray	*Synthesizing Evaluation: Perspectives, Practices, and Evidence*	William Shadish	Task force to create *Guiding Principles* is formed.
1993	David Fetterman	*Empowerment Evaluation*		Development of the evaluation training directory.
1994	Karen Kirkhart	*Evaluation and Social Justice*		*New Directions for Program Evaluation* becomes *New Directions for Evaluation*.
				Task force on minority issues is formed.
				Guiding Principles for Evaluators is published.
				Second edition of *Joint Committee Standards for Program Evaluation* is published.

Year				
1995	Eleanor Chelimsky	*Evaluation for a New Century: A Global Perspective*	Lois-ellin Datta	Joint meeting with the Canadian Evaluation Society in Vancouver, British Columbia.
				EvalTalk created.
1996	Leonard Bickman	*AEA: A Decade of Progress: Looking Back and Looking Forward*		Best Evaluation award created.
1997	William Shadish	*Theory and Practice: Partners in Evaluation*		Management firm hired to run AEA. *Evaluation Practice* becomes *American Journal of Evaluation*.
1998	Donna Mertens	*Transforming Society Through Evaluation*	Gary Henry and Jennifer Greene	AEA's role in internationalizing evaluation is formalized.
				The Building Diversity Initiative begins.
				Management firm fired; conference management assumed by Susan Kistler.
1999	Michael Scriven	*The Territory Ahead*		Scriven managed AEA after management firm was fired.
2000	Laura Leviton	*Evaluation Capacity Building*		AEA management taken over by Susan Kistler.
				Kellogg and NSF grants to support Building Diversity Initiatives.
2001	James Sanders	*Mainstreaming Evaluation*		Electronic newsletter implemented.
				First AEA task force (high-stakes testing).
2002	Molly Engle	*Evaluation—A Systematic Process That Reforms Systems*		Review of the *Guiding Principles* initiated.
				Updated survey of evaluation preparation programs.

(continued)

Table 1.1. *Continued*

Year	President	Annual Conference Theme	NDE Editor-in-Chief	Notable Events
2003	Richard Krueger	*Methodology*	Jean King	The role of board committees is formalized.
				AEA statement on the U.S. Department of Education definition of scientifically based evaluation methods.
2004	Nick Smith	*Fundamental Issues*		AEA monograph series created.
				First class of interns AEA/Duquesne diversity initiative.
				Susan Kistler is appointed executive director of AEA.
2005	Sharon Rallis	*Crossing Borders, Crossing Boundaries*		Joint meeting with the Canadian Evaluation Society, Toronto, Ontario.
2006	Melvin Mark	*The Consequences of Evaluation*		Membership gets online access to *Evaluation Review and Evaluation and Health Professions*.
				History of AEA project begins.
				Creation of a summer institute in conjunction with the Centers for Disease Control.

in the second decade. Notably, six issues focused specifically on evaluation in the public sector, primarily at the federal level, although one issue focused on evaluation and state legislatures.

Although many methods-focused NDE issues have included a chapter that sets the theoretical stage for the "how-to" and "illustrations of" chapters, only a few issues have been primarily devoted to theoretical discussions, ones that describe big or foundational ideas in the field. These issues focus on topics like social justice, reasoning in evaluation, and the philosophical underpinnings of particular evaluation approaches (for example, realist, participatory, and democratic evaluation). An equally small number of issues have focused on the profession of evaluation, discussing topics such as how evaluators are or should be educated (four issues), codes of ethics and professional practice (three issues), and forms of professional evaluation practice (one issue).

Parallel to the focus of NDE issues are themes selected for the AEA annual meetings over this same time span. Table 1.1 summarizes this information, also indicating who the association presidents and NDE editors-in-chief have been over the past two decades, and highlights some, although not all, key events during the AEA's maturation as a professional association. Most of these data are from the AEA history project and are derived from a session at the 2006 AEA annual meeting in Portland. All but a few of the past presidents participated in this session, with a summary by Hallie Preskill, 2007 association president. In her summary, Preskill likened AEA's development to the stages of human development, moving through childhood and adolescence to its current state of adulthood. If in the first twenty years AEA was developing a sense of identity and purpose, in its adulthood it will likely turn to domains associated with adult growth, such as affective, moral, and consciousness development. AEA's past presidents opined in the question-and-answer portion of the session that the likely future directions of the association ought to include a focus on evaluators' public responsibility, including participation in policy debates and decisions. The next twenty years will tell.

SANDRA MATHISON is professor of education at the University of British Columbia and editor-in-chief of New Directions for Evaluation.

NEW DIRECTIONS FOR EVALUATION • DOI: 10.1002/ev

2

This chapter provides a brief history of New Directions
for Evaluation—*how the journal came into being, key
events in the life of the journal, and its purpose.*

A Short History of *New Directions for Evaluation*

Lois-ellin Datta

New Directions for Evaluation (NDE) and the *American Journal of Evaluation*
are the two official publications of the American Evaluation Association.
The editors of each are appointed by the AEA Board. The publications
represent the professional excellence sought by the association and fulfill
one of AEA's missions in promoting the development of evaluation as a field.
The contents are consistent broadly with the policies, practices, and standards of AEA.

Conceived as a sourcebook, in which an issue or approach can be examined in more depth than it could be in a journal article, *New Directions in
Evaluation* began under the editorship of Scarvia Anderson, with its roots
in the national conventions of the Evaluation Research Society, which later
joined in 1986 with the Evaluation Network to become AEA. Many panel
discussions at these meetings had outstanding presentations. At the time,
there were books on evaluation but no refereed evaluation journals, and there
was an expressed need for a monograph-length, relatively fast publication.
The periodical was called *New Directions for Program Evaluation* at the beginning, but Michael Scriven successfully argued for a more inclusive journal
title, a change that started with issue 68, *"Reasoning in Evaluation,"* edited by
Deborah Fournier.

This chapter is reprinted with permission from L. Datta, "New Directions for Evaluation."
In S. Mathison (ed.), *Encyclopedia of Evaluation.* Thousand Oaks, Calif.: Sage, 2004.

NEW DIRECTIONS FOR EVALUATION, no. 114, Summer 2007   © Wiley Periodicals, Inc.
Published online in Wiley InterScience (www.interscience.wiley.com) • DOI: 10.1002/ev.222

For many years, NDE has been a refereed publication. A proposal for an issue, which must be on a single topic with contributions organized by the guest editor or editors, is sent to the editors-in-chief of NDE. The proposal is in a sense a mini-issue, presenting a comprehensive discussion of the proposed theme and its justification. Summaries of the proposed chapters by the prospective authors are extensive and complete. Proposals in turn receive thorough written reviews, according to the established protocol, by several (usually four to six) members of the Editorial Board. The proposal additionally may be reviewed by relevant substantive experts. This permits fairly detailed interaction between issue editors and the editors-in-chief, helping to ensure the quality and relevance of the issue. The guest editor and the editors-in-chief also review the final manuscript before its publication and distribution by Jossey-Bass.

Over the past 15 years, more than 100 issues of NDE have been published, under the guidance of editors-in-chief that have included Scarvia Anderson, Ronald Wooldridge, Ernest House, Mark Lipsey, Nick Smith, Willam Shadish, Lois-ellin Datta, Jennifer Greene, and Gary Henry. The first issue, edited by Scarvia Anderson and Claire Coles, was *"Exploring Purposes and Dimensions,"* followed by Charlotte and Robert Rentz's *"Evaluating Federal Programs."* Subsequent topics have included (a) forums on methodology and theory, such as evaluation models, secondary analysis, survey research, and qualitative and quantitative methods; (b) examinations of the intersection of evaluation and broader social questions, such as multicultural evaluation, evaluation as a democratic process, and diversity in evaluation; (c) shared experiences and lessons learned—sometimes rueful, sometimes encouraging—such as experiences with control group designs in evaluation and in conducting multisite evaluations in real-world settings; and (d) presentation of newer approaches, such as the use of templates in evaluation, program theory, and appreciative inquiry.

Shorter than a book, much longer than an article, NDE has provided a forum for empirical, methodological, and theoretical work in evaluation. The common thread is a reflective approach, seeking balance and examination of a topic, more than advocacy for (or against) issues in these three broad areas.

LOIS-ELLIN DATTA is president of Datta Analysis. She was editor-in-chief of NDE from 1995 to 1997.

NEW DIRECTIONS FOR EVALUATION • DOI: 10.1002/ev

3

This chapter situates Guba and Lincoln's chapter within the broad philosophical debate about the justifiability of interpretations.

Judging Interpretations

Thomas A. Schwandt

Among the most knotty problems faced by investigators committed to interpretive practices in disciplines and fields such as sociocultural anthropology, jurisprudence, literary criticism, historiography, feminist studies, public administration, policy analysis, planning, educational research, and evaluation are deciding whether an interpretation is credible and truthful and whether one interpretation is better than another. Several contested epistemological issues make this problem particularly complex and very difficult both to understand and to solve (Bohman, Hiley, and Shusterman, 1991). First is the claim that interpretation is an omnipresent feature of all human attempts to understand—in other words, there can be no appeal to some kind of evidence, experience, or meaning that is somehow outside of interpretation, independent of it, or more basic than it. To put it more directly, an interpretivist would say there is no such thing as the "interpretation" of the value of some policy or program, on the one hand, and "evidence" of the value of that policy or program, on the other hand, with the latter being more basic than the interpretation or in some way independent of the interpretation. Although, of course, evidence does matter, the very act of generating evidence or identifying something as evidence is itself an interpretation. Second is the interpretivists' claim that every interpretation is made in some context or background of beliefs, practices, or traditions. This does not necessarily mean that every interpretation is, therefore, subjective (that is, the product of the personal view of the interpreter). In fact, it means just the opposite—namely, there is always an intersubjective aspect of interpretation; the investigator cannot help but always be situated relative to (and cannot escape) social circumstances such as a web of beliefs, practices, standpoints,

and the like that he or she has learned as ways of living and grasping the world (as expressed by Joseph Rouse, 1987). Third, a consequence of these two assertions is the notion that if interpretations are always made in a context or background of shared (social) beliefs and practices, it follows that interpretations are, in an important sense, infused with political and ethical implications related to matters of power and authority. In other words, interpretation is not simply an individual cognitive act but a social and political practice. Clearly, these central principles of a philosophy of interpretivism stand in sharp contrast to what is, more or less, a standard epistemological account of establishing the objectivity and truthfulness of claims that we make about the world. On that account, a claim is considered objective and true to the extent that it is free of any biasing influence of context or background beliefs and accurately mirrors the way the world really is.

It is against this backdrop (and fairly fearlessly entering into this complicated epistemological matter) that Egon Guba and Yvonna Lincoln offered their thinking on the question of appropriate criteria for judging evaluations as interpretations. In the chapter that appears on the following pages (Guba and Lincoln, 1986) and in the two very influential books that serve as bookends to it (Guba and Lincoln, 1985, 1989), they built an argument for the way those committed to the interpretive practice of evaluation could profitably address the difficult problem of demonstrating the credibility of their interpretations. To their credit, as is apparent in the following chapters as well as in the aforementioned books, they did not offer their way of thinking as the last word but rather as an invitation to further debate and consideration. For those of us who have, in the past twenty years, subsequently wrestled with the problem of the nature and justification of interpretations, their work has remained a touchstone for both disagreement on the part of some scholars and elaboration and extension on the part of others in many fields of study. They should be happy that the invitation they issued has been accepted.

What they describe in the chapter are two approaches to thinking about the problem of justifying interpretations. One way they characterize as that of employing *trustworthiness* criteria, and they describe these criteria as analogs to "scientific" understandings of conventional notions of internal validity (*credibility*), external validity (*transferability*), reliability (*dependability*), and objectivity (*neutrality*). The second way, they argue, is fundamentally different, and more aligned with assumptions about interpretations as socially constructed undertakings with significant implications for the ways in which we inevitability use those interpretations to continue to go on with one another (as Wittgenstein might have said)—that is, in making sense of or understanding one another and subsequently acting with confidence on those understandings. Thus, they offered a new (and sometimes difficult) language of *authenticity* criteria—fairness, ontological authenticity, educative authenticity, and catalytic authenticity.

To my way of thinking, although perhaps not to theirs and others, these two ways of approaching the knotty problem of justifying interpretations as credible and truthful are not opposed; in fact, they are complementary. To illustrate, consider the following "evaluative" case: My brother and I have an elderly mother whose everyday life is made more stressful and complicated because she is experiencing progressive dementia and living with a husband who is legally blind. As elderly siblings do with each other, I find myself in the position of evaluating my brother's response to that situation: Is he doing the right thing for our mother and her husband? On the one hand, anyone looking in on that situation would ask whether I really understand the situation and his interactions with them: Do I have the facts of the matter straight? How would I make such assurances of the credibility of my interpretations to an onlooker? I might point out that I have witnessed their interactions firsthand for quite some time and heard both him and my parents describe the situation (persistent observation and prolonged engagement), and that I have asked how others privy to their interactions have sized up his behavior and responses (triangulation), that I have done my best to find evidence that contradicts my interpretation (search for negative cases)—all of these actions leading to some assurances of the credibility, dependability, and confirmability of my interpretations about the value and appropriateness of his responses to the situation. I might develop a story of the way he interacts with them and tell it to others who find themselves in the same situation with elderly parents as a way of demonstrating that there is something to be learned here (transferability).

Yet surely, on the other hand, anyone looking in on this situation would ask some other questions about what happened in the process of my forming an interpretation of the value of my brother's way of dealing with the situation. For example, they might ask whether I really have a balanced view of his reactions: Have I taken into account what my parents think? Have I taken into account my own ways of thinking about what it is right to do in this situation (fairness)? Second, they might ask whether I actually discussed my evolving interpretations of the situation with my brother and whether either of us came to better understand and appreciate (although not necessarily agree with) each other's way of thinking and acting (educative authenticity). Third, an onlooker might ask whether the understandings developed through the sharing of our interpretations of the situation substantially challenged both his and my self-understandings, and whether either of us, as a result of our conversation, was not simply moved to some new or different understanding of the situation at hand but actually began to act differently (catalytic and tactical authenticity).

I leave it to readers to extend by analogy this way of thinking to a more complicated evaluative case they have encountered. Guba and Lincoln's approaches to how we might profitably think about justifying the credibility and truthfulness of the interpretations we make in the interpretive practice of evaluation (and nursing, public administration, planning, cultural anthropology, and so on) are an extension of the ways we support the truth-fulness, honesty, correctness, and actionability of our interpretations in everyday life. To successfully defend our interpretations we appeal to criteria of both trustworthiness and authenticity. Guba and Lincoln name these ways in shorthand expressions befitting our ways of thinking of social scientific practices like evaluation; yet, be not misled, more importantly they have invited us to think more carefully about what judging the credibility of interpretations actually entails in both our everyday lives and our professional lives as interpreters of human actions.

References

Bohman, J. F., Hiley, D. R., and Shusterman, R. "Introduction: The Interpretive Turn." In D. R. Hiley, J. F. Bohman, and R. Shusterman (eds.), *The Interpretive Turn: Philosophy, Science, Culture* (pp. 1–16). Ithaca, N.Y.: Cornell University Press, 1991.

Guba, E. G., and Lincoln, Y. S. *Naturalistic Inquiry*. Thousand Oaks, Calif.: Sage, 1985.

Guba, E. G., and Lincoln, Y. S. "But Is It Rigorous? Trustworthiness and Authenticity in Naturalistic Evaluation." In D. Williams (ed.), *Naturalistic Evaluation*. New Directions for Evaluation, no. 30. San Francisco: Jossey-Bass, 1986.

Guba, E. G., and Lincoln, Y. S. *Fourth Generation Evaluation*. Thousand Oaks, Calif.: Sage, 1989.

Rouse, J. *Knowledge and Power*. Ithaca, N.Y.: Cornell University Press, 1987.

THOMAS A. SCHWANDT is professor of education at the University of Illinois, Urbana-Champaign. He earned his Ph.D. in inquiry methodology at Indiana University, Bloomington, where Egon Guba was his thesis director.

The emergence of a new paradigm of inquiry (naturalistic) has, unsurprisingly enough, led to a demand for rigorous criteria that meet traditional standards of inquiry. Two sets are suggested, one of which, the "trustworthiness" criteria, parallels conventional criteria, while the second, "authenticity" criteria, is implied directly by new paradigm assumptions.

But Is It Rigorous? Trustworthiness and Authenticity in Naturalistic Evaluation

Yvonna S. Lincoln, Egon G. Guba

Until very recently, program evaluation has been conducted almost exclusively under the assumptions of the conventional, scientific inquiry paradigm using (ideally) experimentally based methodologies and methods. Under such assumptions, a central concern for evaluation, which has been considered a variant of research and therefore subject to the same rules, has been how to maintain maximum rigor while departing from laboratory control to work in the "real" world.

The real-world conditions of social action programs have led to increasing relaxation of the rules of rigor, even to the extent of devising studies looser than quasi-experiments. Threats to rigor thus abound in sections explaining how, when, and under what conditions the evaluation was conducted so that the extent of departure from desired levels of rigor might be judged. Maintaining true experimental or even quasi-experimental designs, meeting the requirements of internal and external validity, devising valid and reliable instrumentation, probabilistically and representatively selecting subjects and assigning them randomly to treatments, and other requirements of sound procedure have often been impossible to meet in the world of schools and social action. Design problems aside, the ethics of treatment given and treatment withheld poses formidable problems in a litigious society (Lincoln and Guba, 1985b).

We are indebted to Judy Meloy, graduate student at Indiana University, who scoured the literature for references to fairness and who developed a working paper on which many of our ideas depend.

D. D. Williams (Ed.). *Naturalistic Evaluation.*
NEW DIRECTIONS FOR PROGRAM EVALUATION, no. 30. San Francisco: Jossey-Bass, June 1986.

15

Given the sheer technical difficulties of trying to maintain rigor and given the proliferation of evaluation reports that conclude with that ubiquitous finding, "no significant differences," is it not surprising that the demand for new evaluation forms has increased. What is surprising—for all the disappointment with experimental designs—is the *continued* demand that new models must demonstrate the ability to meet the same impossible criteria! Evaluators and clients both have placed on new-paradigm evaluation (Guba and Lincoln, 1981; Lincoln and Guba, 1985a) the expectation that naturalistic evaluations must be rigorous in the conventional sense, despite the fact that the basic paradigm undergirding the evaluation approach has shifted.

Under traditional standards for rigor (which have remained largely unmet in past evaluations), clients and program funders ask whether naturalistic evaluations are not so subjective that they cannot be trusted. They ask what roles values and multiple realities can legitimately play in evaluations and whether a different team of evaluators might not arrive at entirely different conclusions and recommendations, operating perhaps from a different set of values. Thus, the rigor question continues to plague evaluators and clients alike, and much space and energy is again consumed in the evaluation report explaining how different and distinct paradigms call forth different evaluative questions, different issues, and entirely separate and distinct criteria for determining the reliability and authenticity—as opposed to rigor—of findings and recommendations.

Rigor in the Conventional Sense

The criteria used to test rigor in the conventional, scientific paradigm are well known. They include exploring the truth value of the inquiry or evaluation (internal validity), its applicability (external validity or generalizability), its consistency (reliability or replicability), and its neutrality (objectivity). These four criteria, when fulfilled, obviate problems of confounding, atypicality, instability, and bias, respectively, and they do so, also respectively, by the techniques of controlling or randomizing possible sources of confounding, representative sampling, replication, and insulation of the investigator (Guba, 1981; Lincoln and Guba, 1985a). In fact, to use a graceful old English cliché, the criteria are honored more in the breach than in the observance; evaluation is but a special and particularly public instance of the impossibility of fulfilling such methodological requirements.

Rigor in the Naturalistic Sense: Trustworthiness and Authenticity

Ontological, epistemological, and methodological differences between the conventional and naturalistic paradigms have been explicated elsewhere (Guba and Lincoln, 1981; Lincoln and Guba, 1985a; Lincoln and Guba, 1986;

Guba and Lincoln, in press). Only a brief reminder about the axioms that undergird naturalistic and responsive evaluations is given here.

The axiom concerned with the nature of reality asserts that there is no single reality on which inquiry may converge, but rather there are multiple realities that are socially constructed, and that, when known more fully, tend to produce diverging inquiry. These multiple and constructed realities cannot be studied in pieces (as variables, for example), but only holistically, since the pieces are interrelated in such a way as to influence all other pieces. Moreover, the pieces are themselves sharply influenced by the nature of the immediate context.

The axiom concerned with the nature of "truth" statements demands that inquirers abandon the assumption that enduring, context-free truth statements—generalizations—can and should be sought. Rather, it asserts that all human behavior is time- and context-bound; this boundedness suggests that inquiry is incapable of producing nomothetic knowledge but instead only idiographic "working hypotheses" that relate to a given and specific context. Applications may be possible in other contexts, but they require a detailed comparison of the receiving contexts with the "thick description" it is the naturalistic inquirer's obligation to provide for the sending context.

The axiom concerned with the explanation of action asserts, contrary to the conventional assumption of causality, that action is explainable only in terms of multiple interacting factors, events, and processes that give shape to it and are part of it. The best an inquirer can do, naturalists assert, is to establish plausible inferences about the patterns and webs of such shaping in any given evaluation. Naturalists utilize the field study in part because it is the only way in which phenomena can be studied holistically and *in situ* in those natural contexts that shape them and are shaped by them.

The axiom concerned with the nature of the inquirer-respondent relationship rejects the notion that an inquirer can maintain an objective distance from the phenomena (including human behavior) being studied, suggesting instead that the relationship is one of mutual and simultaneous influence. The interactive nature of the relationship is prized, since it is only because of this feature that inquirers and respondents may fruitfully learn together. The relationship between researcher and respondent, when properly established, is one of respectful negotiation, joint control, and reciprocal learning.

The axiom concerned with the role of values in inquiry asserts that far from being value-free, inquiry is value-bound in a number of ways. These include the values of the inquirer (especially evident in evaluation, for example, in the description and judgment of the merit or worth of an evaluand), the choice of inquiry paradigm (whether conventional or naturalistic, for example), the choice of a substantive theory to guide an inquiry (for example, different kinds of data will be collected and different interpretations made in an evaluation of a new reading series, depending on whether the evaluator follows a skills or a psycholinguistic reading theory), and contextual values (the values inhering in the context, and which, in evaluation, make a remarkable difference in how evaluation findings may be accepted and used). In addition, each of these four value sources will interact with all the others to produce value resonance or dissonance. To give one example, it would be equally absurd to evaluate a skills-oriented reading series naturalistically as it would to evaluate a psycholinguistic series conventionally because of the essential mismatch in assumptions underlying the reading theories and the inquiry paradigms.

It is at once clear, as Morgan (1983) has convincingly shown, that the criteria for judging an inquiry themselves stem from the underlying paradigm. Criteria developed from conventional axioms and rationally quite appropriate to conventional studies may be quite inappropriate and even irrelevant to naturalistic studies (and vice versa). When the naturalistic axioms just outlined were proposed, there followed a demand for developing rigorous criteria uniquely suited to the naturalistic approach. Two approaches for dealing with these issues have been followed.

Parallel Criteria of Trustworthiness. The first response (Guba, 1981; Lincoln and Guba, 1985a) was to devise criteria that parallel those of the conventional paradigm: internal validity, external validity, reliability, and objectivity. Given a dearth of knowledge about how to apply rigor in the naturalistic paradigm, using the conventional criteria as analogs or metaphoric counterparts was a possible and useful place to begin. Furthermore, developing such criteria built on the two-hundred-year experience of positivist social science.

These criteria are intended to respond to four basic questions (roughly, those concerned with truth value, applicability, consistency, and neutrality), and they can also be answered within naturalism's bounds, albeit in different terms. Thus, we have suggested credibility as an analog to internal validity, transferability as an analog to external validity, dependability as an analog to reliability, and confirmability as an analog to objectivity. We shall refer to these criteria as criteria of trustworthiness (itself a parallel to the term *rigor*).

Techniques appropriate either to increase the probability that these criteria can be met or to actually test the extent to which they have been met have been reasonably well explicated, most recently in Lincoln and Guba (1985a). They include:

For credibility:

- Prolonged engagement—lengthy and intensive contact with the phenomena (or respondents) in the field to assess possible sources of distortion and especially to identify saliencies in the situation
- Persistent observation—in-depth pursuit of those elements found to be especially salient through prolonged engagement
- Triangulation (cross-checking) of data—by use of different sources, methods, and at times, different investigators

- Peer debriefing—exposing oneself to a disinterested professional peer to "keep the inquirer honest," assist in developing working hypotheses, develop and test the emerging design, and obtain emotional catharsis
- Negative case analysis—the active search for negative instances relating to developing insights and adjusting the latter continuously until no further negative instances are found; assumes an assiduous search
- Member checks—the process of continuous, informal testing of information by soliciting reactions of respondents to the investigator's reconstruction of what he or she has been told or otherwise found out and to the constructions offered by other respondents or sources, and a terminal, formal testing of the final case report with a representative sample of stakeholders.

For transferability:

- Thick descriptive data—narrative developed about the context so that judgments about the degree of fit or similarity may be made by others who may wish to apply all or part of the findings elsewhere (although it is by no means clear how "thick" a thick description needs to be, as Hamilton, personal communication, 1984, has pointed out).

For dependability and confirmability:

- An external audit requiring both the establishment of an audit trail and the carrying out of an audit by a competent external, disinterested auditor (the process is described in detail in Lincoln and Guba, 1985a). That part of the audit that examines the process results in a dependability judgment, while that part concerned with the product (data and reconstructions) results in a confirmability judgment.

While much remains to be learned about the feasibility and utility of these parallel criteria, there can be little doubt that they represent a substantial advance in thinking about the rigor issue. Nevertheless, there are some major difficulties with them that call out for their augmentation with new criteria rooted in naturalism rather than simply paralleling those rooted in positivism.

First, the parallel criteria cannot be thought of as a complete set because they deal only with issues that loom important from a positivist construction. The positivist paradigm ignores or fails to take into account precisely those problems that have most plagued evaluation practice since the mid 1960s: multiple value structures, social pluralism, conflict rather than consensus, accountability demands, and the like. Indeed, the conventional criteria refer only to methodology and ignore the influence of context. They are able to do so because by definition conventional inquiry is objective and value-free.

Second, intuitively one suspects that if the positivist paradigm did not exist, other criteria might nevertheless be generated directly from naturalist assumptions. The philosophical and technical problem might be phrased thus: Given a relativist ontology and an interactive, value-bounded epistemology, what might be the nature of the criteria that ought to characterize a naturalistic inquiry? If we reserve the term *rigor* to refer to positivism's criteria and the term *reliability* to refer to naturalism's parallel criteria, we propose the term *authenticity* to refer to these new, embedded, intrinsic naturalistic criteria.

Unique Criteria of Authenticity. We must at once disclaim having solved this problem. What follows are simply some strong suggestions that appear to be worth following up at this time. One of us (Guba, 1981) referred to the earlier attempt to devise reliability criteria as "primitive"; the present attempt is perhaps even more aboriginal. Neither have we as yet been able to generate distinct techniques to test a given study for adherence to these criteria. The reader should therefore regard our discussion as speculative and, we hope, heuristic. We have been able to develop our ideas of the first criterion, fairness, in more detail than the other four; its longer discussion ought not to be understood as meaning, however, that fairness is very much more important than the others.

Fairness. If inquiry is value-bound, and if evaluators confront a situation of value-pluralism, it must be the case that different constructions will emerge from persons and groups with differing value systems. The task of the evaluation team is to expose and explicate these several, possibly conflicting, constructions and value structures (and of course, the evaluators themselves operate from some value framework).

Given all these differing constructions, and the conflicts that will almost certainly be generated from them by virtue of their being rooted in value differences, what can an evaluator do to ensure that they are presented, clarified, and honored in a balanced, even-handed way, a way that the several parties would agree is balanced and even-handed? How do evaluators go about their tasks in such a way that can, while not guaranteeing balance (since nothing can), at least enhance the probability that balance will be well approximated?

If every evaluation or inquiry serves some social agenda (and it invariably does), how can one conduct an evaluation to avoid, at least probabilistically, the possibility that certain values will be diminished (and their holders exploited) while others will be enhanced (and their holders advantaged)? The problem is that of trying to avoid empowering at the expense of impoverishing; all stakeholders should be empowered in some fashion at the conclusion of an evaluation, and all ideologies should have an equal chance of expression in the process of negotiating recommendations.

Fairness may be defined as a balanced view that presents all constructions and the values that undergird them. Achieving fairness may be accomplished by means of a two-part process. The first step in the provision of fairness or justice is the ascertaining and presentation of different value and belief systems represented by conflict over issues. Determination of the actual belief system that undergirds a position on any given issue is not always an easy task, but exploration of values when clear conflict is evident should be part of the data-gathering and data-analysis processes (especially during, for instance, the content analysis of individual interviews).

The second step in achieving the fairness criterion is the negotiation of recommendations and subsequent action, carried out with stakeholding groups or their representatives at the conclusion of the data-gathering, analysis, and interpretation stages of evaluation effort. These three stages are in any event simultaneous and interactive within the naturalistic paradigm. Negotiation has as its basis constant collaboration in the evaluative effort by all stakeholders; this involvement is continuous, fully informed (in the consensual sense), and operates between true peers. The agenda for this negotiation (the logical and inescapable conclusion of a true collaborative evaluation process), having been determined and bounded by all stakeholding groups, must be deliberated and resolved according to rules of fairness. Among the rules that can be specified, the following seem to be the absolute minimum.

1. A negotiation must have the following characteristics:
   a. It must be open, that is, carried out in full view of the parties or their representatives with no closed sessions, secret codicils, or the like permitted.
   b. It must be carried out by equally skilled bargainers. In the real world it will almost always be the case that one or another group of bargainers will be the more skillful, but at least each side must have access to bargainers of equal skill, whether they choose to use them or not. In some instances, the evaluator may have to act not only as mediator but as educator of those less skilled bargaining parties, offering additional advice and counsel that enhances their understanding of broader issues in the process of negotiation. We are aware that this comes close to an advocacy role, but we have already presumed that one task of the evaluator is to empower previously impoverished bargainers; this role should probably not cease at the negotiation stage of the evaluation.
   c. It must be carried out from equal positions of power. The power must be equal not only in principle but also in practice; the power to sue a large corporation in principle is very different from the power to sue it in practice, given the great disparity of resources, risk, and other factors, including, of course, more skillful and resource-heavy bargainers.
   d. It must be carried out under circumstances that allow all sides to possess equally complete information. There is no such animal, of course, as "complete information," but each side should have the same information, together with assistance as needed to be able to come to an equal understanding of it. Low levels of understanding are tantamount to lack of information.

    e. It must focus on all matters known to be relevant.

    f. It must be carried out in accordance with rules that were themselves the product of a pre-negotiation.

2. Fairness requires the availability of appellate mechanisms should one or another party believe that the rules are not being observed by some. These mechanisms are another of the products of the pre-negotiation process.

3. Fairness requires fully informed consent with respect to any evaluation procedures (see Lincoln and Guba, 1985a, and Lincoln and Guba, 1985b). This consent is obtained not only prior to an evaluation effort but is continually renegotiated and reaffirmed (formally with consent forms and informally through the establishment and maintenance of trust and integrity between parties to the evaluation) as the design unfolds, new data are found, new constructions are made, and new contingencies are faced by all parties.

4. Finally, fairness requires the constant use of the member-check process, defined earlier, which includes calls for comments on fairness, and which is utilized both during and after the inquiry process itself (in the data collection-analysis-construction stage and later when case studies are being developed). Vigilant and assiduous use of member-checking should build confidence in individuals and groups and should lead to a pervasive judgment about the extent to which fairness exists.

    Fairness as a criterion of adequacy for naturalistic evaluation is less ambiguous than the following four, and more is known about how to achieve it. It is not that this criterion is more easily achieved, merely that it has received more attention from a number of scholars (House, 1976; Lehne, 1978; Strike, 1982, see also Guba and Lincoln, 1985).

    Ontological Authentication. If each person's reality is constructed and reconstructed as that person gains experience, interacts with others, and deals with the consequences of various personal actions and beliefs, an appropriate criterion to apply is that of improvement in the individual's (and group's) conscious experiencing of the world. What have sometimes been termed *false consciousness* (a neo-Marxian term) and *divided consciousness* are part and parcel of this concept. The aim of some forms of disciplined inquiry, including evaluation (Lincoln and Guba, 1985b) ought to be to raise consciousness, or to unite divided consciousness, likely via some dialectical process, so that a person or persons (not to exclude the evaluator) can achieve a more sophisticated and enriched construction. In some instances, this aim will entail the realization (the "making real") of contextual shaping that has had the effect of political, cultural, or social impoverishment; in others, it will simply mean the increased appreciation of some set of complexities previously not appreciated at all, or appreciated only poorly.

    Educative Authentication. It is not enough that the actors in some contexts achieve, individually, more sophisticated or mature constructions, or those that are more ontologically authentic. It is also essential that they come to appreciate (apprehend, discern, understand)—not necessarily like or agree with—the constructions that are made by others and to understand how those constructions are rooted in the different value systems of those others. In this process, it is not inconceivable that accommodations, whether political, strategic, value-based, or even just pragmatic, can be forged. But whether or not that happens is not at issue here; what the criterion of educative validity implies is increased understanding of (including possibly a sharing, or sympathy with) the whats and whys of various expressed constructions. Each stakeholder in the situation should have the opportunity to become educated about others of different persuasions (values and constructions), and hence to appreciate how different opinions, judgments, and actions are evoked. And among those stakeholders will be the evaluator, not only in the sense that he or she will emerge with "findings," recommendations, and an agenda for negotiation that are professionally interesting and fair but also that he or she will develop a more sophisticated and complex construction (an emic-etic blending) of both personal and professional (disciplinary-substantive) kinds.

How one knows whether or not educative authenticity has been reached by stakeholders is unclear. Indeed, in large-scale, multisite evaluations, it may not be possible for all—or even for more than a few—stakeholders to achieve more sophisticated constructions. But the techniques for ensuring that stakeholders do so even in small-scale evaluations are as yet undeveloped. At a minimum, however, the evaluator's responsibility ought to extend to ensuring that those persons who have been identified during the course of the evaluation as gatekeepers to various constituencies and stakeholding audiences ought to have the opportunity to be "educated" in the variety of perspectives and value systems that exist in a given context.

By virtue of the gatekeeping roles that they already occupy, gatekeepers have influence and access to members of stakeholding audiences. As such, they can act to increase the sophistication of their respective constituencies. The evaluator ought at least to make certain that those from whom he or she originally sought entrance are offered the chance to enhance their own understandings of the groups they represent. Various avenues for reporting (slide shows, filmstrips, oral narratives, and the like) should be explored for their profitability in increasing the consciousness of stakeholders, but at a minimum the stakeholders' representatives and gatekeepers should be involved in the educative process.

Catalytic Authentication. Reaching new constructions, achieving understandings that are enriching, and achieving fairness are still not enough. Inquiry, and evaluations in particular, must also facilitate and stimulate action. This form of authentication is sometimes known as feedback-action validity. It is a criterion that might be applied to conventional inquiries and evaluations as well; although if it were virtually all positivist social action, inquiries and evaluations would fail on it. The call for getting "theory into action"; the preoccupation in recent decades with "dissemination" at the national level; the creation and maintenance of federal laboratories, centers, and dissemination networks; the non-utilization of evaluations; the notable inaction subsequent to evaluations that is virtually a national scandal—all indicate that catalytic authentication has been singularly lacking. The naturalistic posture that involves all stakeholders from the start, that honors their inputs, that provides them with decision-making power in guiding the evaluation, that attempts to empower the powerless and give voice to the speechless, and that results in a collaborative effort holds more promise for eliminating such hoary distinctions as basic versus applied and theory versus practice.

Tactical Authenticity. Stimulation to action via catalytic authentication is in itself no assurance that the action taken will be effective, that is, will result in a desired change (or any change at all). The evaluation of inquiry requires other attributes to serve this latter goal. Chief among these is the matter of whether the evaluation is empowering or impoverishing, and to whom. The first step toward empowerment is taken by providing all persons at risk or with something at stake in the evaluation with the opportunity to control it as well (to move toward creating collaborative negotiation). It provides practice in the use of that power through the negotiation of construction, which is joint emic-etic elaboration. It goes without saying that if respondents are seen simply as "subjects" who must be "manipulated," channeled through "treatments," or even deceived in the interest of some higher "good" or "objective" truth, an evaluation or inquiry cannot possibly have tactical authenticity. Such a posture could only be justified from the bedrock of a realist ontology and an "objective," value-free epistemology.

Summary

All five of these authenticity criteria clearly require more detailed explication. Strategies or techniques for meeting and ensuring them largely remain to be devised. Nevertheless, they represent an attempt to meet a number of criticisms and problems associated with evaluation in general and naturalistic evaluation in particular. First, they address issues that have pervaded evaluation for two decades. As attempts to meet these enduring problems, they appear to be as useful as anything that has heretofore been suggested (in any formal or public sense).

Second, they are responsive to the demand that naturalistic inquiry or evaluation not rely simply on parallel technical criteria for ensuring reliability. While the set of additional authenticity criteria might not be the complete set, it does represent what might grow from naturalistic inquiry were one to ignore (or pretend not to know about) criteria based on the conventional paradigm. In that sense, authenticity criteria are part of an inductive, grounded, and creative process that springs from immersion with naturalistic ontology, epistemology, and methodology (and the concomitant attempts to put those axioms and procedures into practice).

NEW DIRECTIONS FOR EVALUATION • DOI: 10.1002/ev

Third, and finally, the criteria are suggestive of the ways in which new criteria might be developed; that is, they are addressed largely to ethical and ideological problems, problems that increasingly concern those involved in social action and in the schooling process. In that sense, they are confluent with an increasing awareness of the ideology-boundedness of public life and the enculturation processes that serve to empower some social groups and classes and to impoverish others. Thus, while at first appearing to be radical, they are nevertheless becoming mainstream. An invitation to join the fray is most cheerfully extended to all comers.

References

Guba, E. G. "Criteria for Assessing the Trustworthiness of Naturalistic Inquiries." *Educational Communication and Technology Journal*, 1981, 29, 75–91.

Guba, E. G., and Lincoln, Y. S. "Do Inquiry Paradigms Imply Inquiry Methodologies?" In D. L. Fetterman (Ed.), *The Silent Scientific Revolution*. Beverly Hills, Calif.: Sage, in press.

Guba, E. G., and Lincoln, Y. S. *Effective Evaluation: Improving the Usefulness of Evaluation Results Through Responsive and Naturalistic Approaches*. San Francisco: Jossey-Bass, 1981.

Guba, E. G., and Lincoln, Y. S. "The Countenances of Fourth Generation Evaluation: Description, Judgment, and Negotiation." Paper presented at Evaluation Network annual meeting, Toronto, Canada, 1985.

House, E. R. "Justice in Evaluation." In G. V. Glass (Ed.), *Evaluation Studies Review Annual, no. 1*. Beverly Hills, Calif.: Sage, 1976.

Lehne, R. *The Quest for Justice: The Politics of School Finance Reform*. New York: Longman, 1978.

Lincoln, Y. S., and Guba, E. G. *Naturalistic Inquiry*. Beverly Hills, Calif.: Sage, 1985a.

Lincoln, Y. S., and Guba, E. G. "Ethics and Naturalistic Inquiry." Unpublished manuscript, University of Kansas, 1985b.

Morgan, G. *Beyond Method: Strategies for Social Research*. Beverly Hills, Calif.: Sage, 1983.

Strike, K. *Educational Policy and the Just Society*. Champaign: University of Illinois Press, 1982.

At the time of publication Yvonna S. Lincoln *was an associate professor of higher education in the Educational Policy and Administration Department, School of Education, the University of Kansas. Egon G. Guba was a professor of educational inquiry methodology in the Department of Counseling and Educational Psychology, School of Education, Indiana University. They have jointly authored two books,* Effective Evaluation *and* Naturalistic Inquiry, *which sketch the assumptional basis for naturalistic inquiry and its application to the evaluation arena. They have also collaborated with others on a third book,* Organizational Theory and Inquiry, *Sage, 1985.*

4

This chapter situates Lipsey's chapter on small theories in the now much-broader literature on program theory, and highlights key contributions like the focus on relevant constructs and causal attributions.

A Big Chapter About Small Theories

Laura C. Leviton

"Theory as Method: Small Theories of Treatments," by Mark W. Lipsey (1993), is one of the most influential and highly cited chapters to appear in *New Directions for Evaluation*. It articulated an approach in which methods for studying causation depend, in large part, on what is known about the theory underlying the program. Lipsey discussed the benefits of this approach in relation to four major issues in evaluating program effectiveness: how to base the research design on *relevant* constructs and variables; how to best *detect* outcomes subsequent to treatment; how to assure that outcomes can be *attributed* to treatment; and how to *interpret* the overall pattern and offer practical implications.

To be sure, several authors have made important contributions to methods designed to elicit program theory and to improve causal inferences based on program theory. Chen and Rossi (1994) were at this time finishing their book on theory-driven evaluation; Cronbach (1982) had long advocated theory-building as a way to enhance both internal and external validity and improve evaluation practice. Wholey (1987) had developed the logic model, in which a basic theory of programs is elicited. Yeaton and Sechrest (1981) had explored the dimensions of the dose-response relationship in program treatments. Two years after the publication of this chapter, the Aspen Institute developed methods for explicating the theory of change for comprehensive community initiatives (Connell, Kubish, Schorr, and Weiss, 1995). Indeed, the seeds of program theory as method can clearly be seen in Suchman's (1967) pioneering evaluation monograph. What, then, was special about Lipsey's exposition?

Lipsey made several unique contributions in this chapter. First, it was astute to call this approach the study of *small theories,* because the term put practitioners at ease and freed evaluators to consider a wide range of constructs and their relationships in framing the evaluation question. The idea of theory intimidates or alienates many practitioners—especially the "big" metatheories of psychology, sociology, and other social science disciplines. All too often these are too abstract and inaccessible for practitioners to employ without some means of bridging to the specific case, the here and now. Also, researchers too often deal with *big theory* without a clear pathway to its explication, use, and adaptation in specific real-world settings. Or researchers may believe they "should" use such metatheories in evaluation. But Lipsey illustrated how "should" depends entirely on the program at hand. The grand metatheories are employed where relevant, but it was helpful to elicit practitioners' and program developers' own theories about how the program should work, and to use these in analysis.

Second, Lipsey drew together several strands of thought concerning the use of theory for a coherent and distinctive approach to evaluation. Lipsey showed us efficient ways to get out of the black box of causal inference, the advantages of doing so, and when and why to do so.

Third, the chapter offered a way to deal with many of the frustrations evaluators experience in coping with poorly operationalized outcome measures, underdeveloped programs, and underpowered studies. The chapter illustrated how an approach that used program theory could address these problems, or at least identify them as they emerged. Good practice could be clearly differentiated from poor practice on this basis. Like Audubon's guide for birding in North America, some of this chapter is a field guide for evaluation to spot the common problems and syndromes of poor practice, and the excellent but, sadly, less common evaluation that chooses relevant measures and design, is sensitive to detecting change, makes sound inferences about cause, and for which interpretation leads to practical implications. Lipsey helped us differentiate the evaluation starlings from the exotic birds.

Some of the statements in the chapter have gained the status of epigrams for the evaluation researcher, things I actually quote to the evaluation client from time to time. Consider the following comment concerning *the relevance of constructs and variables.* It is partly tongue in cheek, but this consideration is tragically absent in much evaluation: "Nothing improves research design so much as having a clear idea about what is being investigated. An important function of theory in research design is to help researchers ensure that they are playing in the right ballpark to begin with—that is, to help them avoid studying the wrong thing (Lipsey, 1993, p. 15).

Concerning the absence of treatment theory in much of evaluation, Lipsey observed: "Over 70 percent of the studies in a representative sample of published treatment effectiveness research offered either no theory or only general statements of the program strategy or principles" (Lipsey, 1993, p. 12).

NEW DIRECTIONS FOR EVALUATION • DOI: 10.1002/ev

No wonder the program is treated as a black box when either the client has not taken the time to specify the relationships between treatment and outcomes, or the evaluator has not bothered to elicit these relationships and operationalize them in the evaluation!

For those of us obsessed with *sensitive detection of change* where it occurs, this chapter is still a major resource. However, it is for the topics of inference and interpretation that Lipsey's recommendations really shine. Of course, Lipsey built on the work of Campbell and Stanley (1966) and Cook and Campbell (1979), who advocated ruling out specific alternative explanations for results—the well-known threats to internal validity. In addition, however, Lipsey returned explicitly to basic social science epistemology to emphasize strong tests of these small theories. A strong test of theory is one in which an explicitly predicted and well-elaborated pattern of data rule out other known alternative explanations. By being very specific about program theory, one can go beyond the conventional quasi-experiments to obtain such strong tests. Thus, Lipsey's work offered new tools for the assessment and interpretation of causal relationships.

As noted, others had contributed to this line of work before, and in many ways. But this very well-written chapter did so in ways that brought many lines of thinking together in a highly useful way.

References

Campbell, D. T., and Stanley, J. C. *Experimental and Quasi-Experimental Designs for Research.* Skokie, Ill.: Rand McNally, 1966.

Chen, H. T., and Rossi, P. H. *Theory-Driven Evaluations.* Thousand Oaks, Calif.: Sage, 1994.

Connell, J., Kubish, A., Schorr, L., and Weiss, C. *New Approaches to Evaluating Community Initiatives: Concepts, Methods, and Contexts.* Washington, D.C.: Aspen Institute, 1995.

Cook, T. D., and Campbell, D. T. *Quasi-Experimentation.* Boston: Houghton Mifflin, 1979.

Cronbach, L. J. *Designing Evaluations of Educational and Social Programs.* San Francisco: Jossey-Bass, 1982.

Lipsey, M. W. "Theory as Method: Small Theories of Treatments." In L. B. Sechrest and A. G. Scott (eds.), *Understanding Causes and Generalizing about Them.* New Directions for Program Evaluation, no. 57. San Francisco: Jossey-Bass, 1993.

Suchman, E. A. *Evaluation Research: Principles and Practices in Public Service and Social Programs.* New York: Russell Sage Foundation, 1967.

Wholey, J. S. "Evaluability Assessment: Developing Program Theory." In L. Bickman (ed.), *Using Program Theory in Evaluation.* New Directions in Program Evaluation, no. 33. San Francisco: Jossey-Bass, 1987.

Yeaton, W. H., and Sechrest, L. B. "Critical Dimensions in the Choice and Maintenance of Successful Treatments: Strength, Integrity, and Effectiveness." *Journal of Consulting and Clinical Psychology,* 1981, *49,* 156–167.

LAURA C. LEVITON is a senior program officer of the Robert Wood Johnson Foundation. She was president of the American Evaluation Association in 2000.

An overview of the critical issues in theory-driven applied research is presented.

Theory as Method: Small Theories of Treatments

Mark W. Lipsey

This chapter examines the role of theory in strengthening causal interpretation in nonexperimental research. It is, therefore, appropriate to begin with a review of some of the fundamentals of causal inference. Following the models of Holland (1986) and Rubin (1974), a population of units can be assumed, in this case persons, each of whom has potential to be exposed to some event, A, and make some response, B. The central question is whether A causes B. Note that this causal question has meaning only when variation can be observed in event A and the response B, and the nature of any correlation can be examined. If A is a constant condition and B is a constant response, there is only tautology in the claim that A causes B—for example, that gravity causes a person to remain on the earth's surface. When circumstances in which A differs can be compared and it is found that B also differs, it is proper to ask if the relationship is causal.

To answer the causal question, researchers capitalize on the inherent comparative nature of the concept of causality. The circumstance when A is present is compared with the circumstance when it is absent in order to observe whether B regularly occurs in the one case and not in the other. This leads to what Holland (1986) and others call the fundamental problem of causal inference. In short, it is physically impossible to compare A-present versus A-absent in otherwise identical circumstances.

A version of this paper was published in L. Sechrest, E. Perrin, and J. Bunker (eds.), *Research Methodology: Strengthening Causal Interpretations of Nonexperimental Data* (Conference proceedings), Washington, D.C.: Agency for Health Care Policy and Research, Public Health Service, U.S. Department of Health and Human Services, May 1990.

The closest alternative is to observe A-present versus A-absent at the same time but on different persons and mount a side argument—in particular, a statistical argument—that there are no important differences among persons. Another option is to observe A-present versus A-absent on the same persons but at different times and argue stability—that is, that there are no important differences among the circumstances occurring at those different times. This point is fundamental. It is what makes causality an inference rather than a fact.

If time could be rolled back and events manipulated as required, causal relations could be established as a matter of observation with the same factual status as any other observation (Reichardt, 1983). In the absence of such ability, it is possible only to approximate the circumstances under which causality can be observed and make informed guesses about the causal relations. Causal analysis thus has a logical component with which causal inference is justified, a methodological component that indicates how to go about approximating the unattainable ideal circumstances for observing causality, and an empirical component that provides the observational facts on which inference is supported in a particular case.

Treatment Theory Versus the Black Box

The premise of this chapter is that all three of the components of causal analysis are importantly and substantially strengthened by an explicit theory about the nature and details of the change mechanism through which the cause of interest is expected to produce the effect(s) of interest. In particular, this chapter is concerned with "treatment theory," which attempts to describe the process through which an intervention is expected to have effects on a specified target population. A closer look at the practical circumstances within which causal analysis is generally done will set the stage for this discussion.

Most situations in which intervention might be attempted can be characterized as "black boxes." Black boxes, as Ashby (1956) defined them, are organisms, devices, or situations for which inputs and outputs can be observed, but the connecting processes are not readily visible. A simple, prototypical black box model is depicted in Figure 4.1.

Black boxes are an apt depiction of many human situations in which an intervention is desirable. Through social action upon various black boxes—that is, through treatments, programs, policies, and the like— various agents seek to influence often-complex problem situations in ways

Figure 4.1. Prototypical Black Box Model

that better the human condition. Within the domain of practical or applied social science, there are two types of interesting situations. In one case, the objective is to manipulate inputs, that is, provide treatments, in order to produce beneficial outputs. The other is the case in which the goal is to identify the causes of dysfunctional outputs, such as undesirable medical, psychological, or social conditions, so that those conditions can be prevented. Methodologically, there are only two general approaches that will support reasonable causal inference. It is possible to manipulate the inputs and observe how outputs are affected, that is, an experiment can be conducted. Or an investigator can observe, but not manipulate, variations in input and attempt to relate those to variation in output—an observational or correlational approach.

In either case, the task of designing causal research is largely a matter of mapping events onto a research paradigm (Chen and Rossi, 1980). That is, the segment of reality that is of interest is mapped or coded into variables and relationships that, in turn, are operationalized as measures (observations) and procedures. In a very literal sense, the research study itself is a model or representation of what are taken to be the important features and relations of the respective reality. Moreover, much of what is meant by "validity" in research has to do with the correspondence or fit between the research representation and the substantive reality of interest (Brinberg and McGrath, 1985).

Ashby's black box provides the minimal generic specification of variables and relationships necessary for causal research. It is necessary only to identify the black box of interest (for example, a target population such as asthmatics), an input to manipulate or observe (for example, ingestion of vitamin B_6), and an outcome of interest (for example, wheezing). Proper observation of subjects' consumption of vitamin B_6 and a reasonable measure of wheezing comprise the rudiments of a study of the causal proposition that vitamin B_6 reduces wheezing in asthmatics.

Comparison of this research paradigm to the segment of reality that it maps reveals that it has simplified and abstracted that reality to a considerable extent. The typical research design does not depend on, or necessarily offer, any description of the causal process at work between the treatment and the outcome—that part is left inside the black box. Moreover, in the experimental version of the paradigm, the treatment is generally applied in molar fashion as an undifferentiated whole present with all its concomitants in one condition and absent in the other. In its minimal form, this research paradigm is almost completely an atheoretical "try this and see if it works" approach. Most treatment effectiveness research in the social sciences is in fact conducted in this minimalist form or close to it (Lipsey and others, 1985), and the situation may not be very different in the medical sciences (Kleinman, 1986).

There can be little quarrel with this minimalist research paradigm when it is applied to relatively simple situations, such as input events that are basically indivisible molar wholes, a few well-defined outcome states, and input-output changes that are contiguous, immediate, and direct. Indeed, it is worth remembering that, in the Fisherian tradition, experimental design was invented for agricultural studies that had many of these properties. However, most causal phenomena of practical interest are more complex. They involve multidimensional interactions that often are extended over time, complex multistep causal processes in which different individuals may react differently, and uncertain and potentially wide-ranging outcomes, not all necessarily desirable.

Clearly, these more complex cases can be, and frequently are, approached in the minimalist black box paradigm. A complex and varying set of ill-defined educational activities, such as the Head Start Program, can be defined as a package, applied to a treatment group, and withheld from a control group. After a reasonable period of time, various outcomes measures can be taken to see if the groups differ. With proper research design, this approach can establish empirical, molar cause-and-effect linkages involving manipulable treatment packages. From a practical standpoint, these treatment packages provide buttons that, when pressed, produce useful effects; it may seem that little more could be desired. Press the planned parenthood button, and the birthrate goes down; press the Sesame Street button, and children's academic proficiency goes up; press the antismoking campaign button, and cancer rates decrease; and so forth. Any policymaker, human services professional, or social do-gooder would be delighted to have all of these buttons identified for practical use.

Despite the appeal of these simple cause-and-effect images, application of the molar black box research paradigm to complex phenomena often underrepresents and oversimplifies to such a degree that the results are crude and distorted depictions of the circumstances investigated. The coding of input as molar categories may obscure its multidimensional character, overlook important variability within the categories, and ignore exogenous variables that may accompany and interact with input. Treatment of the causal relationship itself as an unexamined process within the black box may make it impossible to understand how it works, what intervening or mediating variables are critical, and what interactions with subject and setting characteristics occur. On the output side, the molar black box paradigm often focuses on a narrow range of dependent variables to the neglect of unexpected side effects, the interrelationships among effects, and the timing, magnitude, and durability of those effects.

The alternative to black box research, of course, is to differentiate the research paradigm in ways that better represent the underlying complexity. Such differentiation results in a research study that more richly represents the details of the causal process of interest. Even more important, it supports the construction of differentiated concepts about the processes involved, which can lead to sophisticated causal theory instead of the simple but vague empirical facts that result from molar black box experimentation on complex causal situations. The Catch-22 for this approach is that meaning-ful differentiation of input, causal process, and output requires that the research begin with a conceptual or theoretical framework on which such differentiation can be based. Any approach to experimental research on treatment effectiveness other than the molar black box approach, therefore, requires the researcher to be theory-oriented. In the bootstrapping pattern so common in science, theory must play a role prior to the research, as a basis for planning, and a role after the research, as a scheme for organiza-tion and interpretation of results and as a target for revision or rejection in the face of those results.

Given the extra burden that theory orientation places on the researcher and the research process, the crucial question is, "What is gained by con-ducting theory-oriented treatment effectiveness research?" In basic research, this is a frivolous question, since theory building is the primary motive of the endeavor. In the practical and applied domain, it is a question that deserves thoughtful consideration. Some answers are itemized below (see also Adelman, 1986; Bickman, 1987; Chen and Rossi, 1980, 1983; Cordray and Lipsey, 1987; Hawkins, 1978; Mark, 1986; Sechrest, 1986a).

Discovery. The molar black box approach to treatment effectiveness research implicitly relies on a trial-and-error process for discovery of promis-ing treatments. Candidate treatments may arise serendipitously, come from an atheoretical "let's try this and see if it works" experimentation, or be developed by practitioners as reflections of their intuition and experience (Campbell, 1986). The up-or-down results of molar black box tests of such treatments give little guidance about how they might be improved or where to look for better tests. At best, a trial-and-error approach is an inefficient way to discover promising treatment approaches. At worst, it floats on the surface of the target problems, testing what seems reasonable or is popular at the moment but not probing into the (possibly counterintuitive) causal heart of the matter. Theory-oriented treatment research, at least as a complement to serendipity and clinical intuition, has the advantages of supporting inferences about new treatment approaches with potential for success and providing a conceptual basis for refining and improving existing treatment.

Research Design. Somewhat paradoxically, theory orientation may have its greatest advantage in the domain of practical research design. The task of studying the effects of complex treatments on complex human beings under relatively uncontrolled field conditions is no easy matter. A theory orientation provides a framework within which the researcher can address the fundamental but vexing questions of which controls to imple-ment, which samples to use, which measures to take, and which procedures to follow. It can help guide the research to designs that have increased prob-ability of detecting treatment effects, permit stronger causal inference, and produce more interpretable and generalizable results. These matters are of such importance to conducting treatment effectiveness research that they are revisited in greater detail later in this chapter.

Knowledge and Application. As Aristotle says in *Metaphysics,* "What we call wisdom has to do with first causes and principles of things." He goes on to say that the masters of a craft are those who know the reasons for the things that are done, the whys and the causes. Such knowledge permits treatment to be applied in an intelligent and responsive fashion rather than in mechanical or stereotyped form. When "the why" and "the cause" are known, an approach can be adapted to varying circumstances. When only the empirical fact is known, the treatment can only be reproduced as ritual in the hope that it will have the expected effects. No matter how numerous, disjointed empirical cause-and-effect facts do not make for knowledge about treatment and the problems that treatment addresses. Knowledge, in contrast to facts, requires theory, that is, a framework of interconnected concepts that gives meaning and explanation to relevant events and supports new insights and problem-solving efforts. Theory-oriented treatment research holds out the promise of increasing knowledge in ways that build the practical science of social intervention while informing policy and practice throughout the helping disciplines.

Nature of Theory in Practical Science

Two kinds of theory are relevant to practical science: theory that models ameliorative processes, such as treatments or programs, and theory that models the processes that produce problems needing amelioration, such as personal or social dysfunctions (Chen and Rossi, 1980). It should be quite clear that these are not the same. Treatment theory deals with the change mechanism through which treatment can have effects on the problem. Problem theory deals with the natural or social causes of the problem. An understanding of how a problem comes about often suggests possible approaches to treatment, but there is no necessity for the processes that produce the problem to play a role in remedying it. A headache, for example, may be produced by tension, dilation of capillaries, and other such factors, while an effective treatment for headache may consist of an analgesic that raises pain thresholds—a connected but different causal process.

Moreover, there is a relationship between the two types of theory and the two methods for investigating causality mentioned earlier. Typically, experimental methodology is restricted to the investigation of treatment effects because it is rarely possible to manipulate directly the inputs that contribute to problem situations. Thus, treatment theory is generally more pertinent for experimental or quasi-experimental investigation than for observational or correlational investigation. The etiology of problem situations, to which problem theory applies, is more likely to be studied using correlational methods.

Although this discussion is restricted to treatment theory and the techniques used to investigate treatment effectiveness, there are strong parallels

NEW DIRECTIONS FOR EVALUATION • DOI: 10.1002/ev

between the role of treatment theory in experimental research and the role of problem theory in correlational research. Much of what can be said about the former also applies to the latter, but no attempt is made here to be explicit about those parallels.

Treatment Theory

Treatment theory is a set of propositions regarding what goes on in the black box during the transformation of input to output, that is, how a bad situation is transformed into a better one through treatment inputs. It is a small theory attempting explanation of specific treatment processes, not a large theory of general social or biological phenomena. Appropriate elements of treatment theory include the following: (1) a problem definition that specifies what condition is treatable, for which populations, and under what circumstances, that is, a statement of boundaries that distinguishes relevant from irrelevant situations; (2) specification of the critical inputs (what is necessary, what is sufficient, and what is optimal to produce the expected effects), the interrelationships among the inputs, and the basis for judging magnitude or strength of inputs (for example, dosage levels); (3) the important steps, links, phases, or parameters of the transformation process that the treatment brings about, the intervening or mediating variables on which the process is contingent, and the crucial interactions with individual differences, timing, mode of delivery, or other relevant circumstances; and (4) specification of the expected output (nature, range, and timing of various treatment effects and side effects) and the interrelationships or contingencies among the outputs.

In addition, treatment theory might well encompass other factors (Bickman, 1987; Chen and Rossi, 1983; Finney and Moos, 1984; Rossi, 1978; Scheirer, 1987; Sechrest, 1986a). For example, there may be (1) exogenous factors, that is, contextual or environmental factors that will significantly affect treatment processes (such as facilities, training of personnel, and social conditions, which may include organizational factors, especially when treatments are embedded in broader programs); (2) implementation issues, that is, aspects of the treatment delivery system relevant to its function of providing the specified treatment; or (3) stochastic factors, that is, probabilistic disturbances of the social, treatment, and research circumstances involved in any program; background variability in events, persons, measures; and so forth.

Several caveats are in order at this point. First, it is counterproductive to approach treatment theory by holding dogmatically to a doctrine. The relationship between treatment theory and research constitutes an iterative process in which theory is subject to refinement and rejection as additional evidence edits theory and as improved theory leads to additional evidence. Second, it is not presumed that research needs to proceed on the basis of a single treatment theory; indeed, many treatment circumstances are so complex that numerous theories are equally plausible (Bickman, 1987; Gottfredson, 1984; McClintock, 1987). Different researchers may use different conceptual frameworks, and a single researcher may entertain multiple working hypotheses (Chamberlin, 1965). Finally, it is not necessary for treatment theory to be elaborate and detailed in order to be useful. It is more important for the theory to be explicit, so that its implications for research design and interpretation can be carefully considered. Relatively little is needed on this score to improve the current state of evaluation practice.

As Lipsey and others (1985) showed, over 70 percent of the studies in a representative sample of published treatment effectiveness research offered either no theory or only general statements of the program strategy or principles. Fewer than 10 percent presented any theoretical context more general than the empirical relations among the variables under investigation, that is, some integrated theory linking program elements, rationale, and treatment processes.

Sources of Treatment Theory

A major handicap for the position espoused in this chapter is the relative lack of readily available and pertinent background theory for most medical, psychological, educational, and social treatments of practical interest. In comparison with the wealth of physical and chemical theory available to an engineer, the social sciences have little to offer, and the health sciences are somewhere in between. Treatment practice, therefore, may run well ahead of treatment theory, that is, very promising treatments may be designed on the basis of the experience and intuition of practitioners with little theoretical structure. Given this state of affairs, other approaches to theory development for treatments must generally be considered. Three such approaches are as follows.

First, make what use is possible of "off-the-shelf" theory from relevant disciplines. Often this will be unsatisfactory, but it may provide a point of departure, if not a usable theoretical framework. At a minimum, previous research on the treatment of interest should be examined; or, for innovations, similar treatments should be examined and relevant concepts identified. Sometimes a theoretical perspective from a different area can be used effectively for a treatment situation. For example, Weinholtz and Friedman (1985) used small group leadership theory as a starting point to orient their study of the effectiveness of teaching by attending physicians in a medical school. A more detailed example is the extensive mapping of social learning theory onto the case of family intervention as a treatment for antisocial children that has been developed over more than a decade at the Oregon Social Learning Center (Patterson, 1986).

Second, develop theory in separate studies prior to the evaluation of the treatment or program. When possible, develop the program on the basis of prior pilot studies that differentiate and test the components of treatment. Wang and Walberg (1983) used this latter approach effectively to design and evaluate a program of "adaptive learning environments" for elementary school students. Starting with relevant theory from cognitive psychology and teaching effectiveness research, they developed, tested, and modified various program components before these components were assembled into a program model and evaluated under field conditions. More generally, this approach might begin with extensive qualitative investigation of the domain of interest to identify important factors and relationships in order both to stimulate theorizing and, more important, to ground it in detailed observation (Glaser and Strauss, 1967).

Third, draw out the theory or theories implicit in any operational program or treatment from program personnel, relevant clinical practitioners, or recipients. In recent years, a number of techniques have been developed for this task (McClintock, 1987). They range from relatively unstructured interview or interaction techniques (Gottfredson, 1984; Wholey, 1987) to very structured scaling and clustering techniques (Bougon, 1983; Trochim, 1983, 1985), with various questionnaire approaches in between (Conrad and Miller, 1987). For example, Gottfredson (1984) described the "program development evaluation approach" in which researchers use organizational development techniques to collaborate with program personnel in identifying problems, setting goals, deriving action theories, and evaluating interventions in an iterative cycle aimed at producing stronger programs and better intervention theory.

Obviously, these approaches are not mutually exclusive, and most require that researchers do a great deal of the theory synthesizing themselves. This demanding task requires, at a minimum, that the researchers have in mind a variety of possible formats within which to express theoretical perspectives on a treatment. It may be instructive to review some of the formats more likely to be appropriate (Lipsey and Pollard, 1989).

Basic Two-Step. The minimal improvement that a researcher might make in a black box representation of the treatment process is to specify the key intervening variables that connect treatment with outcome, thereby defining a simple two-step treatment theory. One step represents the assumption that program operations actually affect the intervening variables; the other step represents the assumption that a change in the identified intervening variables will result in a change in the target outcome variables. For example, Chandler (1973) identified social egocentrism as an important mediating factor in juvenile delinquency and designed an intervention based on the training of role-taking skills. The evaluation results showed an increase in role-taking ability, the mediating variable, and a corresponding decrease in delinquency.

Causal Diagram. A familiar way to depict causal processes is through a causal diagram that identifies important variables (as boxes or labels) and their causal influences (as arrows) on one another. The causal diagram may be an informal sketch of the variables identified and relationships hypothesized, or it may be a more carefully defined "model" for input into structural equation analysis (Judd and Kenny, 1981). Rossi, Berk, and Lenihan (1980) used this approach to model the effects of paying unemployment benefits to released felons. This format highlighted the possibility of opposing causal processes: decreased economic hardship with potential for lowering criminal activity versus work disincentive effects with potential for raising it. Judd and Kenny (1981) offered a simpler example in their illustration of the causal links in the Stanford Heart Disease Prevention Project. Their causal analysis hypothesized that the treatment (mass media and personal instruction) would affect knowledge about dietary factors associated with heart disease risk, which in turn would lead to changes in dietary practices that would yield changes in levels of serum cholesterol and triglyceride in the blood.

Stage-State Analysis. Many program and treatment processes can be conceptualized most easily in terms of the various stages and states through which clients progress—and occasionally regress—under the influence of treatment (Brownell, Marlatt, Lichtenstein, and Wilson, 1986). Where the causal diagram works with variables and causal arrows, the stage-state analysis works with categories and transition probabilities (Runyan, 1980). Caplan's (1968) analysis of the interaction of juveniles with street gang workers demonstrates the basic framework. Caplan classified the progress of each juvenile into eight stages. Early stages were related to the youth's participation in program activities; later stages represented the therapeutic relationship with the counselor and, finally, the autonomy of changed behavior. For each stage, a juvenile could be in one of four states: not yet at the stage, at the stage, regressed from the stage to an earlier stage, or passed beyond the stage. With this framework, Caplan was able to categorize the developmental path of each juvenile through the program and produce insights into many aspects of the treatment process.

A similar approach focusing more on organizational categories and statuses was taken by Taber and Poertner (1981) in a study of a large child care system. They were able to show that changed client status was more a function of the organization than of the behavior of either the client or the treatment professional.

Substantive Model. Treatment processes that deal with physical or biological mechanisms often can be modeled in substantive terms. That is, a specific physical or physiological mechanism is described in terms of its components and processes, and the treatment effects are mapped onto that mechanism. This is the type of theory that describes how a clock works, how hormones affect eating behavior, and how dialysis works for victims of kidney failure.

Role of Theory in Method

The foregoing has made a general case for the use of theory in treatment effectiveness research, described what is meant by theory, and provided guidance on how to develop theory. The stage is set for the major focus of this chapter: detailed consideration of the role of theory in treatment evaluation methodology. To provide an organizational framework for discussion, this topic is considered in relation to each of four crucial issues in treatment effectiveness research.

First, the research design must be based on relevant constructs and variables. Second, the important outcomes that occur subsequent to treatment must be detected. Third, those outcomes must be attributable to the treatment. Fourth, the overall pattern of results must be interpretable and have practical implications.

The central argument developed here is that consideration of each of these issues is substantially aided by treatment theory. Advice is offered on the effective use of treatment theory as a methodological tool. Of particular interest is the important role of theory in quasi-experimental research, where the lack of controls increases the ambiguity of the results.

Problem Specification. Nothing improves research design so much as having a clear idea about what is being investigated. An important function of theory in research design is to help researchers ensure that they are playing in the right ballpark to begin with, that is, to help them avoid studying the wrong thing. In the planning stages, all research must begin with a statement of the research question to be investigated and a corresponding identification of the relevant constructs and issues. On this basis, the methodological approach is chosen (for example, experimental, correlational, or descriptive), variables are specified and operationalized, and research procedures are planned. The role of theory in identifying the constructs and relationships relevant to a research problem can be illustrated by examining four aspects of research planning.

Global Plausibility. As Chen and Rossi (1983) point out, many treatments and programs are simply not plausible, either from a common-sense standpoint or on the basis of existing knowledge. They give the example of the 1968 Federal Firearms Regulation Act, which assumed, implausibly, that criminals obtain their guns from commercial dealers, that dealers can recognize prohibited persons who attempt a purchase, and that registration records can easily be used to trace gun ownership. The research frame for implausible treatments should of necessity be different from that for plausible treatments. Given the likelihood that the treatment will prove ineffective, the research should make special effort to identify faulty assumptions and document their deficiencies. Potentially, it would be even more useful to develop an alternate treatment theory applicable to the same context and incorporate an assessment of its assumptions into the research.

Even when a treatment is plausible, the research can benefit from an application of alternate theoretical perspectives to the treatment circumstances in an effort to identify important constructs. For example, psychotherapy could be examined in terms of the constructs salient in the clinical literature and also in terms of persuasion or attitude change processes that might highlight a different set of constructs (see McClintock, 1987, for other examples of multiple perspectives).

Independent-Variable Issues. The researcher must decide how to represent the treatment—that is, the independent variable—in the research. The conventional approach is to encode only one aspect of treatment, whether or not it was present as a molar whole. However, in bringing a theoretical analysis to the treatment, one can reveal numerous other aspects that may be worth considering, especially in the case of complex treatments. For example, it will almost always be relevant to have some idea of the continuum of strength of treatment (Sechrest and others, 1979), in other words, the dosage level at which the treatment is implemented. If treatment strength is low relative to the target problem, little in the way of positive results can be expected. A reasonable approach may be a parametric study in which various dosage levels are implemented and compared. This may be a straightforward approach with pharmaceutical treatments, where the dosage continuum is largely a matter of quantity and frequency, but it may require careful analysis in other contexts. What, for example, is the dosage continuum for medical instruction, physical therapy, family planning counseling, or psychotherapy (Howard, Kopta, Krause, and Orlinsky, 1986)? For complex treatments, it may be questionable whether a single dimension of treatment strength is adequate to represent the treatment construct. Datta (1976) suggests that it may be necessary to use an explicitly multidimensional representation of the treatment. For example, it may be possible to break the treatment down into activities or components (Bickman, 1985) in order to consider their individual contributions to treatment effects and their interactions with each other.

A further complication is that with all but the simplest treatments there is considerable potential for the effects of treatment to interact with characteristics of the treatment delivery system (Rossi, 1978), such as the resources available and the skill and motivation of staff. To represent this situation, the researcher needs a clear distinction between the delivery system and the treatment, as well as an analysis of where they interact. One simple construct frequently applicable to the delivery system is its integrity (Yeaton and Sechrest, 1981), that is, the extent to which the treatment plan is implemented. A strong treatment poorly implemented cannot be expected to have effects, but this interaction will not be apparent to the researcher who does not distinguish between treatment strength and treatment integrity.

Datta (1976) suggests various ways of handling the implementation issue, such as restricting the research to well-implemented treatments, blocking different implementation levels together so that differences among levels can be compared, and defining a measurable implementation continuum that can be used as a variable in the analysis. In all cases, some measure or index of implementation is required, which necessitates identification of the constructs along which important variation in implementation can take place (Rezmovic, 1984; Scheirer and Rezmovic, 1983).

Subject Issues. Without clear specification of the problem that the treatment is expected to remedy and, more particular, the target population, treatment effectiveness research has considerable potential for misrepresentation. Target groups that do not have the problem or are not at risk for the problem obviously cannot be helped by treatment, no matter how effective. The task of defining the target population is not problematic in cases where there are relatively straightforward, observable, and unambiguous symptoms to provide criteria. In other cases, however, adequate definition requires a framework of concepts about the nature of the problem and its observable manifestation in the target population.

Consider, for example, juvenile delinquents as a target population for remedial treatment. At first blush, it would seem very easy to define this group. Usually, they are identified according to their arrest records. It is now known, however, that most juveniles who are arrested by the police are not chronic delinquents and, furthermore, that most chronic delinquents are not arrested by the police (Dunford and Elliott, 1984; Elliott, Dunford, and Huizinga, 1986). Therefore, researchers who are studying treatments for delinquency face a considerable challenge in specifying the symptoms or indicators that identify the population for whom treatment is appropriate. Without some prior understanding and a framework of appropriate constructs, such identification may be virtually impossible (Loeber and Stouthamer-Loeber, 1987).

Given a definition of the target population, another set of issues comes into play. Can that population be expected to be homogeneous with regard to characteristics that interact with treatment effectiveness? Some treatments, like being hit on the head with a baseball bat, affect everyone about the same. Others, like psychotherapy, are apt to have varying effects depending on the circumstances and characteristics of each recipient. In the latter cases, there are a variety of subpopulations for whom treatment-outcome relationships may differ. Failure to distinguish among them misrepresents treatment effects and muddies an understanding of the nature of treatment benefits. To find such patterns of differential response, measures must be included for those subject characteristics likely to interact with treatment. This, in turn, requires a conceptual framework within which such relations can be hypothesized. Miller (1985) illustrates such a framework with his thorough review of the important role of motivational variables in treatment entry, compliance, and outcome for alcoholics and other addicts. For these populations, resistance to treatment plays a major role in the relationship between program inputs and outputs (Snowden, 1984); failure to account for this treatment resistance leads to ambiguous research results, whatever the outcome.

Dependent-Variable Issues. Chen and Rossi (1980) argue that every program disturbs the targeted social system to some extent and thus has some effects, though possibly trivial. The challenge for evaluation research is to know which effects are important and to be able to detect them. Perhaps the most important, yet most neglected, function of theory in

treatment research is its capacity to aid the researcher in specifying the constructs or variables on which change can reasonably be expected as a result of a given treatment, that is, specification of which behaviors, states, conditions, and so forth are likely to be affected. Without this specification, there is little basis for selection of outcomes measures and little assurance that the measures selected are appropriate. Even a researcher who elects to proceed on a black box basis with regard to treatment inputs needs specification of the expected outcomes. Independent variables can be manipulated, permitting the researcher some control even without a close understanding of the nature of the variables. Dependent variables, however, must be anticipated and measured, which inescapably requires specification of the constructs to be represented in the measures.

There are at least three aspects of the specification of outcome variables, each requiring some a priori theory, even if only at the level of hunches and hypotheses. However, the better the theory, the better is the resulting specification of expected outcomes. First, a researcher must know what construct domains are subject to change as a result of a given treatment (which behaviors, states, conditions, and so on are likely to be affected). The more complex the treatment program, the more uncertainty there is about the range and nature of possible outcomes. As has been widely noted, the official statements of treatment goals are typically too vague to provide adequate research guidance or, at best, are limited to comments about a select few target benefits expected. Other possible outcomes, such as adverse side effects or unintended benefits, are rarely anticipated in official program goals (or may be specifically excluded; see O'Sullivan, Burleson, and Lamb, 1985, on evaluation of cutbacks in renal dialysis services). While a broad, unconstrained search for such unintended effects (for example, the "goal-free evaluation" of Scriven, 1974) can be advocated, the possibilities are limitless, and practicality requires that the domain be narrowed in some reasonable manner, for example, on the basis of some treatment theory that provides guidance (Sherrill, 1984).

Although important, identification of the construct domains within which effects are considered possible only amounts to development of a set of labels or variable names. A crucial and widely underappreciated next step is specification of the operational details of the measures that will represent those constructs in the research design. This step requires very close specification of the nature of expected effects, and it relies heavily on some conceptual framework, whether implicit or, far better, explicit. The following examples illustrate the nature of the issues at this stage of research.

One neglected aspect in the selection of operational measures is the extent to which measures that appear to be only slightly different can yield different results. Of necessity, the researcher must be clear about which outcome aspect is most important to measure. Consider, for example, a simple learning outcome of an education intervention. Are the effects to be manifest primarily as knowledge (in other words, operationally, the student can explain the subject matter), as application (the student can appropriately apply knowledge to new situations), or as recognition (the student recognizes correct answers)? Measures based on these different operationalizations will be less than perfectly correlated and may yield different results.

Datta (1976) cites an evaluation in which an expected program outcome was greater "career maturity." "Career attitude" was the measure used, and according to the test developer, it was not synonymous with "career maturity." This type of slippage is all too common in evaluation research.

Other operational details of outcome measures also need to be informed by a theory of expected effects. For example, Shapiro (1984b) raises the issue of the distribution of effects. As Shapiro points out, in terms of the expected effect of an education program, there is a great deal of difference among raising the achievement level of every recipient, raising the level of those initially lowest and thus most disadvantaged, and decreasing the discrepancies between the most advantaged and the least advantaged.

The timing of measures is also important. Many studies measure dependent variables at the conclusion of treatment with perhaps one follow-up. This approach implies a model in which effects have an abrupt onset and peak immediately after treatment, but other models of effects are clearly possible. For example, effects could peak early in treatment and then decline, or there could be large "sleeper" effects, little effects at the end of treatment but much larger effects later. Also, there might be different timing for different outcome variables, with some effects most pronounced immediately after treatment and others at some later time. The choice of appropriate times for outcomes measurement requires an explicit and well-justified model of the nature of the expected effects and the points at which they are expected to appear. In the absence of such a model, it is quite possible that even with careful research, an investigator will fail to detect important treatment effects simply by looking in the wrong place at the wrong time.

A final issue involves knowing what constitutes a meaningful outcome once adequate measurement has been operationalized. Here, at least two facets of the problem require some underlying framework or theory. First, the centrality of the result (Datta, 1976) is at issue. Some outcomes are more important than others, and good research should reflect a clear comprehension of which is which. Second, the practical significance of any effect found is at issue, that is, the size of effect that would be meaningful in the context of the treatment and target problem.

It is widely acknowledged that an effect can be statistically significant but not practically significant (the reverse is also possible, of course). Identification of appropriate criteria for judging practical significance requires some concept of the problem situation (Datta, 1980; Sechrest and Yeaton, 1981). For example, the effects of remedial programs might be judged according to the extent to which they closed the gap between the disadvantaged and the "normal" population. Alternatively, some quality-of-life framework might be invoked in which posttreatment conditions would be compared with a minimal set of standards for personal functioning (Baker and Intagliata, 1982). Without such a framework, measured outcomes remain at the operational and statistical level and cannot be retranslated into their implications for the original constructs of interest in the treatment or problem context.

Statistical Detection of Effects. After the treatment, subjects, and outcomes measures are specified, attention is directed to the ability of the planned research to detect whatever treatment effects are present. It is increasingly clear that a major shortcoming of much practical treatment research is inadequate statistical power that yields null results even when the treatment is genuinely effective (Cohen, 1982; Lipsey and others, 1985; Rossi and Wright, 1984; Schneider and Darcy, 1984). A low probability of detecting treatment effects originates in a combination of common circumstances. Often there are limited numbers of subjects available for research, and, among those who do participate, attrition rates can be high. In addition, under field conditions, treatment may be implemented inconsistently or at reduced strength, and data collection and measurement may be subject to various disturbances that lower reliability (Boruch and Gomez, 1977; Lipsey, 1983).

Statistical power is a function of the effect size to be detected, the sample size, the alpha level set by the researcher (conventionally, $p < .05$), and the type of statistical test employed. The last two factors offer limited opportunity for improvement. Of course, the most straightforward approach to increasing statistical power is to use larger samples. Since it is often not possible to obtain the optimal number of subjects under practical conditions, researchers may sweep the power issue under the rug, assuming that there is nothing else to be done. In fact, there are effective strategies available for increasing statistical power without necessarily increasing sample size (Lipsey, 1990). However, many of these strategies depend on assumptions about the treatment process and the subjects' reactions to it.

If the number of subjects is constrained, the only remaining parameter is effect size. Although effect size (always some variation on percentage of dependent-variable variance accounted for by the independent variable) may appear to be a fixed value for a given treatment or research context, many of the factors that determine effect size can be constructively influenced by the researcher (Sechrest and Yeaton, 1982). To illustrate this point, two factors that greatly influence effect size are considered: the sensitivity of the dependent measures to the treatment effect and the extent to which the "error" variance on the dependent variable can be controlled.

Measurement Sensitivity. Outcomes measures that are responsive to treatment-induced change yield comparatively large effects and, hence, increased statistical power. The sensitivity of a dependent measure is a function of a number of factors, including construct validity, ceiling and floor effects, and the units in which it is scaled. Most important, measurement sensitivity is a matter of how closely the measure is keyed to the specific nature of the change expected. At issue in the measurement response to change is whether the measure is to be oriented to the overall level of performance after treatment or to the amount of change in performance occurring over the pretreatment to posttreatment interval.

For example, suppose the treatment of interest is elementary school arithmetic instruction, in particular, the teaching of fractions. The effects of such teaching could be measured in two different ways. In one approach, the students would be given a mathematics achievement test appropriate to their grade level. If they have received effective instruction, their scores should increase on such a test. Note, however, that the increase will be incremental, and many other factors, including natural aptitude and prior learning, also will be reflected in the scores. The net result is that the difference between a group receiving instruction and a group that does not will be only a small portion of the full range of scores.

The second approach is more similar to what the teacher is likely to do, that is, give a test on fractions. A test that is carefully focused on the content of the relevant instructional domain can be expected to be much more responsive to instructional effects. It is quite possible that all students in a group not receiving instruction would score virtually zero on such a test, while all those with instruction would score virtually 100 percent. In this case, the group difference is not incremental but represents nearly the full range of scores on the measure. This example contrasts psychometric measures with criterion-referenced measures (Carver, 1974), but the issue is somewhat more general. Any treatment effect can be looked at in terms of the specific changes that are expected to take place or in terms of the broader content or performance domain within which the changes are to occur. A measure focused on the changes will generally show considerably larger effects than will a measure focused on the broader domain. Selection of a measure without consideration of this issue can greatly affect the research outcome. When the early Head Start researchers expected cognitive gains in target children and, largely for convenience, selected intelligence quotient (IQ) measures (which, by definition, are not supposed to change), they almost guaranteed that negligible effects would be found. When a program to decrease aggressive behavior among adolescents uses police arrest rates as a dependent variable, a similar choice is made (Lipsey, 1983).

Though measurement sensitivity is clearly important to the ability of treatment research to detect effects, this issue cannot be approached without at least rudimentary treatment theory. The selection of measures focused on the specific changes expected from treatment requires a relatively detailed model of just what change process the treatment induces. Similarly, selection of appropriate measures for the broader domain within which change takes place also requires careful clarification of the nature of that domain and its relevance as an arena for treatment effects.

Error Control. The effect size parameter in statistical power compares the difference between treatment and control group means to the within-groups variability. Any procedure that reduces the within-groups variability will increase effect size and, therefore, statistical power. Thus, a given difference between a treatment and a control group will be statistically significant if the variance within the groups on the pertinent measure is sufficiently small, and insignificant if that variance is sufficiently large.

The source of variation in dependent variables is of interest to the researcher who is attempting to improve statistical power. The potential sources are numerous; indeed, any factor that differentially affects the scores across subjects contributes to this variance. Familiar sources of this so-called error variance that are at least partially under the researcher's control include the reliability of the measures used, the consistency of the experimental procedures, and the subject-sampling strategies. (While important, the rationale for these factors is drawn almost entirely from concepts of statistical theory and research design that cannot be pursued here.) At least three other factors that are relevant to error variance can be used effectively only when guided by treatment theory. One such factor is the natural heterogeneity of subjects on the dependent variables prior to treatment, that is, the different baseline values from which different subjects begin. Such differences become part of the error term for statistical significance testing. If subjects are relatively homogeneous, a smaller difference between treatment and control group is required for statistical significance. One straightforward approach to controlling for this source of variance is to administer pretests on the variables of interest, which are then entered as covariates or blocking factors in the analysis of posttest values. Pretests are not always feasible, however, and other covariates may be used (for example, sex, age, socioeconomic status, and IQ). Such covariates are effective only to the extent that they are related to the dependent variables of interest. The selection of appropriate covariates requires an understanding of the nature of the dependent variables and the pattern of relationships in which they are involved for the target population; these are elements of what is called treatment theory. IQ, for example, is generally a good stand-in variable for initial differences on academic achievement tests because of its theoretical and empirical links with that performance domain.

A similar situation occurs when there is likelihood of differential subject response to treatment, that is, when treatment does not increase every subject's score by a constant increment. If some subjects react more strongly than others on the dependent-variable dimensions, that variability will inflate the value of the error term and reduce the overall treatment-control contrast to an average that obscures the uneven effects of treatment on different subjects. The only way to distinguish such variability from other sources of error so that it can be removed from the analysis is by identifying those subject variables that are related to the extent of response to treatment and including them in the statistical model as covariates or blocking factors that interact with the treatment-outcome relationship. For example, in a study of brief inpatient psychiatric treatment, Smith, Cardillo, and Choate (1984) found that the outcome for male veterans had a complex relationship to age: Patients treated during adult developmental transition periods improved the most.

The effects of differential response to treatment on ability to detect treatment effects were shown in even more striking form by Crano and Messe (1985). When they applied standard analytical techniques to data from a complex energy conservation intervention, they found no effects. A refined analysis, however, showed that the treatment had considerable impact on those whose comprehension of the treatment contingencies was high, but this effect was lost when all subjects were analyzed together.

Another source of differential subject response is differential treatment. That is, the treatment may lack integrity in that some subjects receive more or less of the treatment, larger or smaller doses, longer or shorter periods of contact, and so on and show proportionately larger or smaller effects. Variability in treatment delivery generally produces variability in the response to treatment. Such variability shows up in the error terms against which the treatment effects are tested.

Degradation of treatment delivery also has the potential of so diluting treatment overall that the main effect is attenuated. Ideally, treatments would be tested under conditions of high strength and integrity in which little variation occurs. For complex treatments, especially when subjects are volunteers, it is often difficult to maintain a constant dose. If the researcher has a workable notion of the important dimensions of treatment strength and integrity, those dimensions can be measured separately and be included in the analysis with the same effect of reducing error variance as a covariate predicting differential subject response. In this case, it is the treatment delivery that is being modeled and not other bases for the subject response. For example, Cook and Poole (1982) demonstrated the increase in statistical power that resulted in an evaluation of a nutrition supplementation program when data on the level of treatment implementation were included directly in the analysis (but see Mark, 1983, for a pertinent caution). The gain in power was attained by the simple technique of using an independent variable to represent treatment as a continuum of degrees rather than as a dichotomy crudely contrasting treatment versus no treatment (see Johnston, Ettema, and Davidson, 1980, for a similar approach).

Refined effect measurement and statistical error control can have appreciable influence on the effect size function in experimental research and a corresponding influence on the statistical power of the design, that is, its ability to detect treatment effects. The use of such refined techniques is, of necessity, dependent on a good understanding of practical statistical theory. In many cases, however, it is equally dependent on a good understanding of treatment processes and the factors with which they interact.

Causal Attribution of Effects

In addition to constructs and measures that reasonably represent the circumstances of interest and sufficient statistical power to detect expected treatment effects, treatment research also must permit whatever effects are found to be attributed to the treatment rather than to some confounding exogenous factor. In the Campbellian framework, this is an issue of internal validity—the ability of the design to discount various rival explanations for apparent treatment effects (Campbell and Stanley, 1966; Cook and Campbell, 1979). Here, the role of theory is especially important; and the more threats to internal validity there are, the more important treatment theory becomes. The contemporary view of quasi experimentation is that it is more a system of logic than a set of techniques (Trochim, 1986a). The terms and the grounds of that logic depend crucially on the articulation of appropriate treatment theory.

As a practical matter, a causal claim is usually justified on the basis of two sets of criteria. First, researchers rely on what Einhorn and Hogarth (1986) call "cues-to-causality," in particular, temporal order (the candidate cause should precede the effect), covariation (changes in the cause should be accompanied by changes in the effect), contiguity (cause and effect should be adjacent in time and space), and congruity (there should be proportionality between the nature and magnitude of the cause and the effect). Second, plausible alternative causes of the effect must be ruled out. This concept is the familiar notion from the Campbellian tradition of quasi experimentation in which various "threats to internal validity" can be enumerated and, in valid design, can be countered item by item. For example, this approach requires a demonstration that differences between treatment and control groups after treatment cannot be accounted for by differences that were present before treatment.

In a randomized experiment conducted in the laboratory, precedence of cause and contiguity of cause and effect are established directly by manipulation of experimental conditions. Covariation and usually congruity are demonstrated when differences in the dependent variables are found for the different experimental groups. Other possible causes can be ruled out in primarily two ways.

First, the random assignment of subjects to experimental conditions provides statistical (probabilistic) assurance that there are no initial differences that could reappear in dependent measures as apparent treatment effects. However, after assignment to conditions, randomization does not exclude variables other than treatment from affecting the dependent variables of interest. Where little time elapses between assignment to conditions, treatment, and dependent-variable measurement, there is little opportunity for other influences to intrude. More generally, however, other influences are ruled out through experimental control of the circumstances. That is, between the point of assignment to groups and the measurement of dependent variables, the experimenter strives to keep the circumstances constant and comparable among experimental conditions in every relevant particular except for the treatment manipulation itself.

Nonexperimental or quasi-experimental designs for investigating treatment effects generally follow the same pattern as true experiments with the exception of randomized assignment of subjects to conditions. Thus, such designs typically provide similar evidence on the criteria of precedence of cause, contiguity, covariation, and congruity, but they allow for the possibility of initial differences among experimental groups that may rival the treatment manipulation as explanations for apparent effects.

The task of designing experimental research that results in evidence that meets the criteria for causal inference is not particularly problematic in cases where the events of interest are readily visible and immediate and where they occur within a well-understood context. To use the standard example, elaborate logic and experimental controls are not needed to conclude that the erosion of an iron bar is caused by the acid in which it is immersed. Precedence of cause, contiguity, covariation, and congruity are established by immediate perception, and everyday knowledge of the characteristics of iron bars indicates the improbability that something else in the context makes them dissolve.

Causal inference becomes much more difficult when the key events are less visible and immediate, familiarity with the factors that commonly cause change in the context is lacking, or it is clear that the effects of interest can be caused by any of a large number of factors in that context. Unfortunately, it is these more difficult inferential circumstances that generally apply to investigation of medical, psychological, educational, and social treatments. For example, psychotherapy as a treatment for depression occurs over an extended time, on more than one occasion, with results that may not appear immediately or primarily on the treatment site and may be incremental and cumulative rather than sudden and dramatic. Moreover, the effects of interest—positive mood changes, improved social functioning, and the like—are commonplace, complex, and not well understood, and they can be brought about by a host of everyday circumstances and life events other than psychotherapy.

Under such circumstances, both sets of criteria for causal inference present problems. Although research may provide evidence for the temporal precedence of cause and for covariation between cause and effect, both contiguity and congruity may be low. That is, effects will not necessarily closely follow purported causes or occur in the same settings, and their form and magnitude may bear no readily visible relation to the form and magnitude of treatment. As for ruling out rival causes, degradations to randomization or the inability to randomize at all, lack of experimental control between treatment administration and measurement of dependent variables, and the typically large number of other possible causes of the effects of interest all undermine the attempt to demonstrate that the treatment is the only plausible source of any effects found.

Good treatment theory can shore up causal inference in cases where method and circumstance result in an insufficient demonstration of causal cues or the implausibility of rival explanations. The following sections examine the roles that theory can play in augmenting cues-to-causality and eliminating rival explanations.

Cues-to-Causality. Where the purported effect comes some time after administration of the causal event, as in the effects of psychotherapy, or is not proportionate or similar to the cause, as in the effects of radiation, the causal claim is weakened by the lack of any obvious connection between cause and effect. If such a connection can be demonstrated, the causal inference gains strength. Good treatment theory provides that linkage. Treatment theory elucidates the causal chain that carries the action of the treatment through to the otherwise remote effect. If the transmission of the cause through the intermediate links can be demonstrated—for instance, by measurement of change in intervening variables—the causal inference is strengthened. Thus, the causal link between cigarette smoking and lung cancer is made more plausible by the demonstration of the presence of carcinogens in the smoke, by the mechanical connection between smoke particles and lung tissue, and by the demonstration of physiological changes in the lungs of laboratory animals exposed to heavy smoke. The causal link between fat in the diet and cancer of the colon, on the other hand, is considerably weaker due to the lack of a known mechanism through which it might work or a demonstration of the crucial intervening links.

Thus, where there is a long or complex causal chain between the commencement of the treatment and the appearance of the outcome, treatment theory that specifies the intermediate stages in the causal sequence can have a particularly persuasive role in connecting treatment with the observed effects. Research that measures those intermediate stages at the appropriate times and shows the expected state in the treatment group and the absence of that state in the control group at each stage presents a very convincing case that it was the treatment process and not something else that eventually produced the outcome of interest.

As Sechrest (1986b) and Trochim (1986b) have observed, it is difficult to find plausible rival explanations for complex theory-based predictions that are confirmed. To be effective, however, such predictions must specify outcomes in some detail (Judd and Kenny, 1981; Rosen and Proctor, 1978); a complex prediction that only implies that the treatment group will outperform the control group would not be convincing. When a treatment process is well understood, it has a characteristic modus operandi (MO) (Scriven, 1974) that can be observed by an astute researcher. Evidence of that MO in the treatment condition and a corresponding lack of that MO in the control condition strengthen the causal inference connecting treatment with outcome.

As Cordray (1986) has emphasized, it is necessary to "rule in" the treatment as a plausible cause to strengthen causal inference in these circumstances. Where the plausibility of the treatment as a cause is very high, as in the example of acid and iron given earlier, other explanations have proportionately more difficulty competing. Conversely, if the treatment is not plausible, even when supported by the research results, other explanations remain credible. Imagine a carefully randomized experiment in which subjects' names, unbeknownst to them, were engraved on iron bars, some of which were subsequently dissolved in acid. Suppose further that those subjects whose bars were dissolved had higher frequencies of accidents in the following six weeks than those whose iron bars were left intact. While there might be no doubt about the validity of the methodology in this experiment, there would almost certainly be questions about the causal attribution. In the absence of a plausible mechanism by which this ferric voodoo might effect accidental events, the empirical evidence would have to be overwhelming before a causal relationship would be accepted.

The act of ruling the treatment in as an explanation for effects has at least one other important facet: knowledge that the treatment was, in fact, administered to the treatment group and not to the control group. This might appear to be an empirical issue, but closer inspection reveals that it is theory-laden. This judgment requires a definite conception of what constitutes treatment and, often equally important, what does not. Where any variation is possible (as is often the case in applied contexts), the judgment requires knowledge of which aspects of the treatment are crucial, that is, which are the active ingredients, which variations on the treatment are considered sufficient to have effects, and so forth. These matters have as much to do with the conception of the treatment as with its operational reality and thus require at least some minimal theoretical framework.

Elimination of Rival Explanations. The ruling out of rival explanations for effects that covary with treatment is partly a matter of evidence and partly a matter of analysis and judgment. It requires identifying rivals, judging their plausibility, and, if plausible, determining what evidence bears on them (Cordray, 1986; Platt, 1964). This endeavor depends on close knowledge of the research circumstances, including the nature of the treatment process and specific context-bound arguments regarding the nature and plausibility of rival explanations. The more explicit and systematic that knowledge, the stronger are the resulting arguments. At this juncture, a differentiated program theory aids considerably in supporting causal inference in treatment research.

At a minimum, a researcher needs sufficient theory to rule out the possibility of spurious results stemming from gross violation of the assumptions of the statistical model within which covariation is analyzed. Some of those assumptions stipulate a particular form of the underlying causal processes (especially for the complex multivariate statistical analysis often required in applied treatment research). For example, relationships are customarily assumed to be linear and recursive (that is, unidirectional causality), and treatment effects are generally assumed to be additive. Therefore, the responsible researcher must postulate or demonstrate the form of certain crucial features of the causal process in order to ensure proper fit of the statistical model—a minimal but essential use of treatment theory.

Treatment theory also plays a role in examining plausible rival explanations that have to do with the initial configuration of experimental groups. In quasi-experimental designs for which there are initial group differences, those differences can only be ruled out as sources of outcome effects if their contribution to the outcome is separately accounted for prior to assessment of treatment effects. In practice, this means developing a statistical model that accounts for the differential selection of subjects into experimental groups, specifies all of the relevant variables on which the groups differ, or depicts the change or growth process that occurs between the point of group assignment and the point at which outcome is assessed (Reichardt, 1979). Given such a model and appropriate measures for the variables that it specifies, statistical adjustments may be possible that will remove the effects of initial differences from the outcome measures. The catch in this procedure is that the models must be well specified (they must contain all the relevant variables) before the procedure is trustworthy (Reichardt and Gollob, 1986). Clearly, identification of the relevant variables can occur only in situations in which the treatment process, including selection for treatment and the interaction of treatment with subject characteristics, is well understood or can be defensibly hypothesized in some detail.

A related matter has to do with "unbundling" of the treatment. Treatment as operationally applied is always a bundle of various components, some having to do with the treatment concept and others having to do with the delivery system, treatment context, and so forth. The result is that there are always rival explanations for apparent treatment effects among the concomitants of treatment. The most famous of these concomitants is the Hawthorne effect, the reaction that subjects have to the knowledge that they are the treatment group in an experiment. In order to rule out treatment concomitants as an explanation for effects, one must demonstrate that the concomitants alone are not sufficient to produce the same effects (for example, via use of a placebo control). This requires a careful analysis of the treatment bundle to distinguish the "real" treatment ingredients from the associated concomitants, a process greatly dependent on a clear conceptualization of the nature of the treatment.

Consider, for example, the continuing controversy over the nature of placebo effects in psychotherapy research. When treatment is conceptualized within the chemotherapy paradigm, where only physical and chemical manipulations count as treatment, placebo effects are artifacts to be controlled. Within the social-psychological paradigm, where communication, interaction, and suggestion are all legitimate treatment elements, placebo effects are important parts of the treatment process (Wilkins, 1986).

Theory also can be helpful, even essential, in ruling out rival explanations that have to do with differential experiences of the treatment group and the control group (other than the treatment itself) after the experiment is launched. For example, communication between the groups may contaminate the comparison, distinctive experiences of one group may alter its responses, or measurement procedures may be changed (Cook and Campbell, 1979). In order to counter such rivals, the researcher must demonstrate that either (1) nothing happened, that is, there was no differential experience other than the treatment itself, or (2) if something did happen, it did not affect the outcome, at least not enough to account for the results. A good understanding of the treatment process helps the researcher to plan studies that anticipate extraneous events that could mimic treatment effects.

For example, Kutchinsky's (1973) classic quasi-experimental analysis of the effect of the liberalization of Danish pornography laws on the incidence of sex crimes worked from a model that connected the type of offender psychology and the likely effect of pornography on the behavior of different offenders, the attitudes of potential victims toward different types of offenses and their propensity to report those offenses, and the attitudes of the police to whom offenses were reported. This model enabled identification of a number of rival explanations for the decrease in recorded offenses and collection of evidence that permitted a judgment on the plausibility of each of those rivals.

Before we leave the topic of causal inference in treatment research, a brief discussion is needed about the ubiquitous problem of subject attrition. With treatments mounted in the field using volunteer subjects—especially complex, long-term treatments—it is almost inevitable that some subjects will drop out or be otherwise unavailable at crucial data collection points (for example, Shapiro, 1984a). Even worse, subjects may cross over from one experimental group to another (Yeaton, Wortman, and Langberg, 1983). The results can be devastating to the integrity of the research design. A carefully randomized design "goes quasi" (becomes a nonequivalent comparison design) the moment there is subject attrition. In such cases, differential attrition—subjects with different characteristics dropping from the treatment versus the control group—provides a rival explanation for whatever effects are found on outcomes measures. There is no ready solution for this vexing problem.

The best that can be done to rule out differential attrition as an explanation for experimental results is to demonstrate that it did not really occur by showing that there were no differences in relevant characteristics between those who remained in the treatment group and those who remained in the control group (St. Pierre and Proper, 1978). Such a demonstration requires identification of the "relevant" characteristics and proper measurement prior to attrition. A relevant characteristic is one that interacts with the treatment process, a matter that should be specified in a good treatment theory.

Where there is differential attrition, the researcher must attempt to adjust for it, as for initial selection differences, so that it cannot account for the effects found. Such adjustments (for example, via analysis of covariance or structural equations) also require specification of the characteristics of subjects that are likely to interact with treatment or, alternatively, that are likely to motivate their attrition from treatment (Rindskopf, 1986). Again, the net result is that the researcher cannot deal effectively with the attrition problem without a good set of hypotheses about the interaction between subjects and treatment conditions.

Interpretation of Results

In practical treatment research, findings in and of themselves often have little value. Instead, their meaning and implications are what matter (Datta, 1980). The interpretation of results is an essential part of the research, and in this phase too treatment theory can play an important role. Two distinctly different cases are considered here: one in which the research produced null results (no evidence of beneficial treatment effects) and another in which the research produced positive results indicating apparent treatment success.

Null results from treatment effectiveness research are distressingly common (Lipsey and others, 1985; Rossi and Wright, 1984) and inevitably raise more questions than they answer. Treatments are not generally subjected to research unless there is reason to believe that they might be beneficial. Null results, therefore, cry out for an explanation. What went wrong? The answer to that question has serious implications for the validity of the treatment concept, the operation of programs that provide the treatment, and any subsequent research done on the treatment. It is most important to interpret the nature of the failure (Suchman, 1967; Weiss, 1972). The first hypothesis that should be considered is that the research failed, not the treatment. Given the difficulty of conducting treatment effectiveness research, it is not implausible that (1) a given research study was statistically underpowered, (2) outcome variables were misspecified or inappropriately or insensitively measured, (3) treatment was confounded with an exogenous suppressor variable, (4) inappropriate statistical adjustments were used to equate nonrandomized groups, or (5) the study fell into any of a host of other pitfalls inherent to treatment effectiveness research. However, null results should not be accepted unless the research circumstances are sufficient to make them credible (for more extensive discussion of this matter, see Sechrest, 1986b; Yeaton, 1986).

If it appears that the null result probably did not arise from methodological failings, attention should turn to the implementation or delivery of the treatment. At issue here is whether the intended treatment was delivered or, if not, whether sufficient treatment was delivered to produce an effect. In practical treatment situations, it is not uncommon for high proportions of the target population to fail to receive treatment, drop out of treatment shortly after it commences, or receive weak, inconsistent, or diluted treatment. The evidence that bears on this issue is found in data that describe the nature and extent of the treatment received by each experimental subject. The role of treatment theory in this instance is to provide a framework that permits judgment about how treatment should be quantified, what constitute appropriate dimensions of strength and integrity, which treatment components or combinations are essential, and so forth.

Only when adequate methodology and adequate treatment implementation are established can null results be interpreted as indicative of failure of the treatment concept or theory. Even then, however, it is not necessarily appropriate to abandon the treatment concept. For complex treatments, some diagnosis of the treatment failure is required. Which step in the expected causal process failed to occur and why? Can it be easily remedied, or was it a fundamental failure? Does the nature of this failure suggest an alternate treatment theory that might be more effective? The answers to such questions are important for movement beyond a treatment failure toward development of better treatment concepts. Treatment theory serves to guide the collection of data that reflect important details of the causal process, and it also serves as the framework within which treatment failure is probed and interpreted. In the case of treatment effectiveness research that results in a finding of beneficial treatment effects, two related matters are of particular interest.

First, for practical purposes, it is important to understand just what, in fact, produced the result. A researcher must be sure that the "active ingredient" in the treatment (those components of the treatment bundle that were responsible for the effect) has been identified. Without that knowledge, an investigator or practitioner can only mechanically reapply the same bundle, hoping for the same effect in each application. Here, the role of treatment theory and its supporting evidence is obvious. Second, limits on generalizability of the effect must be established. As Campbell (1986) has argued, this is primarily a matter of determining which other situations are similar to the research situation in crucial ways. This kind of analysis requires the researcher to know on which parameters of the research situation the results are contingent. If, for example, the researcher knows that the treatment interacts with subject characteristics of a certain sort, a judgment can be made about whether it will be successful among various target populations that differ on those characteristics. If it is known that the treatment is relatively unaffected by variations in the delivery system, there can be greater confidence that implementation at another site will yield comparable results. As noted earlier, good treatment theory identifies the dimensions on which important variability might occur and permits their inclusion in the research.

Implications of a Theory Orientation for Treatment Research

To guide and integrate method with theory in treatment effectiveness research and thus to gain the benefits described in this chapter, a type of research is required that is different in many ways from what is now conventional. There is the obvious necessity of developing treatment theory to describe what goes on inside the black box between treatment inputs and outputs. Theory must come from somewhere, however, and the most appropriate source is prior research and familiarity with the phenomena involved in a given treatment situation. Thus, theory-guided treatment research must be programmatic and cumulative in the conceptual sense; present practices are more aptly characterized as cumulations of studies conducted in relative independence from one another.

Perhaps more striking is the highly differentiated and multivariate research plan that must accompany this style of research. The simple one-shot, independent-variable/dependent-variable experiment that coincides well with the generic black box depiction of cause-and-effect relations is empirically meager as well as conceptually thin by the standards of theory-oriented treatment research. Instead, such research must be characterized by a host of preliminary studies and side studies and by a highly differentiated measurement scheme going well beyond an independent variable and a few dependent variables. Preliminary studies may be necessary to develop a basis for theory, address issues of dosage or treatment strength, identify appropriate covariates, explore the properties of various candidate measures, and so forth. Side studies may be necessary to address rival hypotheses, unbundle treatment components, examine selection or attrition events, and the like. A highly differentiated measurement scheme is necessary to give the researcher sufficient data on the details of the methods, the treatment implementation, the treatment process, and the expected and unexpected outcomes, so that all of the essential details can be represented and the final results of the study can be properly understood and interpreted.

Obviously, not all treatment effectiveness research must be conducted in this mode. There is a case to be made for testing promising treatments as molar wholes (in other words, black boxes) and exploring the details only after determining that they do have beneficial effects (Campbell, 1986). This reasoning applies more persuasively to simple treatments, since with complex treatments the task of designing research capable of detecting effects and determining the reasons for failure requires relatively detailed advance hypothesizing about the treatment process. More likely, research will lie somewhere between the extremes of the highly differentiated theory-oriented style and the crude, overly simplistic black box style. Even a small step, such as hypothesizing a few intervening variables or mediating processes to come between treatment input and output, and measuring and testing for their role, would greatly improve the research on many complex treatments.

Concluding Recommendations

It is fitting to conclude this chapter with a set of recommendations for the development of treatment theory:

1. Define the problem exactly, specifying its etiology if possible, its magnitude, why it is not self-limiting, where or in what persons or groups it occurs, and its consequences.

2. Define the treatment in terms of what are presumed to be the specific effective ingredients. Formulate a concept of strength of treatment and specify the range within which the planned treatment is likely to lie and the minimal regimen or operationalization necessary to deliver that treatment at effective strength.
3. Describe the mechanisms by which the planned treatment is supposed to have its effects. Specify any variables that are expected to mediate the effects of the treatment and the sequence of steps expected to occur between initial application of the treatment and the occurrence of its effects.
4. Define the desired outcomes as precisely as possible. Specify the minimal magnitudes of effects thought to be interesting, the maximal magnitude thought to be likely, and the timing with which such effects are expected to occur.

Finally, I offer a guided fantasy: Imagine a research community in which every report of a treatment effectiveness study includes a section labeled "treatment theory," which is considered as obligatory as the customary introduction, methods, results, and discussion sections. This chapter is intended to suggest just how much difference it might make to the validity of treatment research if this fantasy became reality.

References

Adelman, M. S. "Intervention Theory and Evaluating Efficacy." *Evaluation Review*, 1986, *10*, 65–83.

Ashby, W. R. *Introduction to Cybernetics*. London: Chapman & Hall, 1956.

Baker, F., and Intagliata, J. "Quality of Life in the Evaluation of Community Support Systems." *Evaluation and Program Planning*, 1982, *5*, 69–79.

Bickman, L. "Improving Established Statewide Programs: A Component Theory of Evaluation." *Evaluation Review*, 1985, *9*, 189–208.

Bickman, L. "The Functions of Program Theory." In L. Bickman (ed.), *Using Program Theory in Evaluation*. New Directions for Program Evaluation, no. 33. San Francisco: Jossey-Bass, 1987.

Boruch, R. F., and Gomez, M. "Sensitivity, Bias, and Theory in Impact Evaluations." *Professional Psychology*, 1977, *8*, 411–434.

Bougon, M. G. "Uncovering Cognitive Maps: The Self-Q Technique." In G. Morgan (ed.), *Beyond Method: A Study of Organization of Research Strategies*. Newbury Park, Calif.: Sage, 1983.

Brinberg, D., and McGrath, J. E. *Validity and the Research Process*. Newbury Park, Calif.: Sage, 1985.

Brownell, K. D., Marlatt, G. A., Lichtenstein, E., and Wilson, G. T. "Understanding and Preventing Relapse." *American Psychologist*, 1986, *41*, 765–782.

Campbell, D. T. "Relabeling Internal and External Validity for Applied Social Scientists." In W.M.K. Trochim (ed.), *Advances in Quasi-Experimental Design and Analysis*. New Directions for Program Evaluation, no. 31. San Francisco: Jossey-Bass, 1986.

Campbell, D. T., and Stanley, J. C. *Experimental and Quasi-Experimental Designs for Research*. Skokie, Ill: Rand McNally, 1966.

Caplan, N. "Treatment Intervention and Reciprocal Interaction Effects." *Journal of Social Issues*, 1968, *24*, 63–88.

Carver, R. P. "Two Dimensions of Tests: Psychometric and Edumetric." *American Psychologist*, 1974, *29*, 512–518.

Chamberlin, T. C. "The Method of Multiple Working Hypotheses." *Science*, 1965, 148 (3671), 754–759.

Chandler, M. J. "Egocentrism and Antisocial Behavior: The Assessment and Training of Social Perspective-Taking Skills." *Developmental Psychology*, 1973, 9, 326–333.

Chen, H. T., and Rossi, P. H. "The Multi-Goal, Theory-Driven Approach to Evaluation: A Model Linking Basic and Applied Social Science." *Social Forces*, 1980, *59*, 106–122.

Chen, H. T., and Rossi, P. H. "Evaluating with Sense: The Theory-Driven Approach." *Evaluation Review*, 1983, 7, 283–302.

Cohen, P. "To Be or Not to Be: Control and Balancing of Type I and Type II Errors." *Evaluation and Program Planning*, 1982, 5, 247–253.

Conrad, K. J., and Miller, T. Q. "Measuring and Testing Program Philosophy: A Framework for Implementation and Evaluation." In L. Bickman (ed.), *Using Program Theory in Evaluation*. New Directions for Program Evaluation, no. 33. San Francisco: Jossey-Bass, 1987.

Cook, T. D., and Campbell, D. T. (eds.). *Quasi-Experimentation: Design and Analysis Issues for Field Settings*. Boston: Houghton Mifflin, 1979.

Cook, T. J., and Poole, W. K. "Treatment Implementation and Statistical Power: A Research Note." *Evaluation Review*, 1982, *6*, 425–430.

Cordray, D. S. "Quasi-Experimental Analysis: A Mixture of Methods and Judgment." In W.M.K. Trochim (ed.), *Advances in Quasi-Experimental Design and Analysis*. New Directions for Program Evaluation, no. 31. San Francisco: Jossey-Bass, 1986.

Cordray, D. S., and Lipsey, M. W. "Evaluation 1986: Program Evaluation and Program Research." In D. S. Cordray and M. W. Lipsey (eds.), *Evaluation Studies Review Annual*. Vol. 11. Newbury Park, Calif.: Sage, 1987.

Crano, W. D., and Messe, L. A. "Assessing and Redressing Comprehension Artifacts in Social Intervention Research." *Evaluation Review*, 1985, *9*, 144–172.

Datta, L. "Does It Work When It Has Been Tried? And Half Full or Half Empty?" *Journal of Career Education*, 1976, 2, 38–55.

Datta, L. "Interpreting Data: A Case Study from the Career Intern Program Evaluation." *Evaluation Review*, 1980, *4*, 481–506.

Dunford, F. W., and Elliott, D. S. "Identifying Career Offenders Using Self-Reported Data." *Journal of Research in Crime and Delinquency*, 1984, *21*, 57–86.

Einhorn, H. I., and Hogarth, R. M. "Judging Probable Cause." *Psychological Bulletin*, 1986, *99*, 3–19.

Elliott, D. S., Dunford, F. W., and Huizinga, D. "The Identification and Prediction of Career Offenders Utilizing Self-Reported and Official Data." In J. D. Burchard and S. N. Burchard (eds.), *The Prevention of Delinquent Behavior*. Newbury Park, Calif.: Sage, 1986.

Finney, J. W., and Moos, R. H. "Environmental Assessment and Evaluation Research: Examples from Mental Health and Substance Abuse Programs." *Evaluation and Program Planning*, 1984, 7, 151–167.

Glaser, B. G., and Strauss, A. L. *The Discovery of Grounded Theory: Strategies of Qualitative Research*. Hawthorne, N.Y.: Aldine, 1967.

Gottfredson, G. D. "A Theory-Ridden Approach to Program Evaluation: A Method for Stimulating Researcher-Implementer Collaboration." *American Psychologist*, 1984, 39, 1101–1112.

Hawkins, D. F. "Applied Research and Social Theory." *Evaluation Quarterly*, 1978, 2, 141–152.

Holland, P. W. "Statistics and Causal Inference." *Journal of the American Statistical Association*, 1986, *81*, 945–960.

Howard, K. L., Kopta, S. M., Krause, M. S., and Orlinsky, D. E. "The Dose-Effect Relationship in Psychotherapy." *American Psychologist*, 1986, *41*, 159–164.

Johnston, I., Ettema, I., and Davidson, T. *An Evaluation of Freestyle: A Television Series to Reduce Sex-Role Stereotypes.* Ann Arbor: Institute for Social Research, University of Michigan, 1980.

Judd, C. M., and Kenny, D. A. "Process Analysis: Estimating Mediation in Treatment Evaluations." *Evaluation Review,* 1981, *5,* 602–619.

Kleinman, A. "Some Uses and Misuses of the Social Sciences in Medicine." In D. W. Fiske and R. A. Schweder (eds.), *Meta-Theory in Social Science: Pluralisms and Subjectivities.* Chicago: University of Chicago Press, 1986.

Kutchinsky, B. "The Effect of Easy Availability of Pornography on the Incidence of Sex Crimes: The Danish Experience." *Journal of Social Issues,* 1973, *29,* 163–181.

Lipsey, M. W. "A Scheme for Assessing Measurement Sensitivity in Program Evaluation and Other Applied Research." *Psychological Bulletin,* 1983, *94,* 152–165.

Lipsey, M. W. *Design Sensitivity: Statistical Power for Experimental Research.* Newbury Park, Calif.: Sage, 1990.

Lipsey, M. W., and Pollard, J. A. "Driving Toward Theory in Program Evaluation: More Models to Choose from." *Evaluation and Program Planning,* 1989, *12,* 317–328.

Lipsey, M. W., and others. "Evaluation: The State of the Art and the Sorry State of the Science." In D. S. Cordray (ed.), *Utilizing Prior Research in Evaluation Planning.* New Directions for Program Evaluation, no. 27. San Francisco: Jossey-Bass, 1985.

Loeber, R., and Stouthamer-Loeber, M. "The Prediction of Delinquency." In H. C. Quay (ed.), *Handbook of Juvenile Delinquency.* New York: Wiley, 1987.

McClintock, C. "Conceptual and Action Heuristics: Program Theory Tools for the Formative Evaluator." In L. Bickman (ed.), *Using Program Theory in Evaluation.* New Directions for Program Evaluation, no. 33. San Francisco: Jossey-Bass, 1987.

Mark, M. M. "Treatment Implementation, Statistical Power, and Internal Validity." *Evaluation Review,* 1983, *7,* 543–549.

Mark, M. M. "What Have We Learned About Studying Causal Process?" Paper presented at the annual meeting of the American Evaluation Association, Kansas City, Missouri, Oct. 1986.

Miller, W. R. "Motivation for Treatment: A Review with Special Emphasis on Alcoholism." *Psychological Bulletin,* 1985, *98,* 84–107.

O'Sullivan, E., Burleson, G. W., and Lamb, W. E. "Avoiding Evaluation Cooptation: Lessons from a Renal Dialysis Evaluation." *Evaluation and Program Planning,* 1985, *8,* 255–259.

Patterson, G. R. "Performance Models for Antisocial Boys." *American Psychologist,* 1986, *41,* 432–444.

Platt, J. R. "Strong Inference." *Science,* 1964, *146* (3642), 347–353.

Reichardt, C. S. "The Statistical Analysis of Data from Non-Equivalent Group Designs." In T. D. Cook and D. T. Campbell (eds.), *Quasi-Experimentation: Design and Analysis Issues for Field Settings.* Skokie, Ill.: Rand McNally, 1979.

Reichardt, C. S. "On the Logic and Practice of Assessing Cause." Paper presented at the annual meeting of the American Educational Research Association, Montreal, Apr. 1983.

Reichardt, C. S., and Gollob, H. F. "Satisfying the Constraints of Causal Modeling." In W.M.K. Trochim (ed.), *Advances in Quasi-Experimental Design and Analysis.* New Directions for Program Evaluation, no. 31. San Francisco: Jossey-Bass, 1986.

Rezmovic, E. L. "Assessing Treatment Implementation amid the Slings and Arrows of Reality." *Evaluation Review,* 1984, *8,* 187–204.

Rindskopf, D. "New Developments in Selection Modeling for Quasi-Experimentation." In W.M.K. Trochim (ed.), *Advances in Quasi-Experimental Design and Analysis.* New Directions for Program Evaluation, no. 31. San Francisco: Jossey-Bass, 1986.

Rosen, A., and Proctor, E. K. "Specifying the Treatment Process: The Basis for Effectiveness Research." *Journal of Social Service Research,* 1978, *2,* 25–43.

Rossi, P. H. "Issues in the Evaluation of Human Services Delivery." *Evaluation Quarterly,* 1978, *2,* 573–599.

Rossi, P. H., Berk, R. A., and Lenihan, K. J, *Money, Work, and Crime: Experimental Evidence.* San Diego: Academic Press, 1980.

Rossi, P. H., and Wright, J. D. "Evaluation Research: An Assessment." *Annual Review of Sociology,* 1984, *10,* 331–352.

Rubin, D. B. "Estimating Causal Effects of Treatments in Randomized and Nonrandomized Studies." *Journal of Educational Psychology,* 1974, *66,* 688–701.

Runyan, W. M. "A Stage-State Analysis of the Life Course." *Journal of Personality and Social Psychology,* 1980, *38,* 951–962.

St. Pierre, R. G., and Proper, E. C. "Attrition: Identification and Exploration in the National Follow-Through Evaluation." *Evaluation Review,* 1978, *2,* 153–166.

Scheirer, M. A. "Program Theory and Implementation Theory: Implications for Evaluators." In L. Bickman (ed.), *Using Program Theory in Evaluation.* New Directions for Program Evaluation, no. 33. San Francisco: Jossey-Bass, 1987.

Scheirer, M. A., and Rezmovic, E. L. "Measuring the Degree of Program Implementation: A Methodological Review." *Evaluation Review,* 1983, *7,* 599–633.

Schneider, A. L., and Darcy, R. E. "Policy Implications of Using Significance Tests in Evaluation Research." *Evaluation Review,* 1984, *8,* 573–580.

Scriven, M. "Maximizing the Power of Causal Investigations: The Modus Operandi Method." In W. J. Popham (ed.), *Evaluation in Education: Current Applications.* Berkeley, Calif.: McCutchan, 1974.

Sechrest, L. B. "Modes and Methods of Personality Research." *Journal of Personality,* 1986a, *54,* 318–331.

Sechrest, L. B. "What Have We Learned About Interpreting No-Difference Findings?" Paper presented at the annual meeting of the American Evaluation Association, Kansas City, Missouri, 1986b.

Sechrest, L. B., and Yeaton, W. H. "Empirical Bases for Estimating Effect Size." In R. F. Boruch, P. M. Wortman, and D. S. Cordray (eds.), *Reanalyzing Program Evaluations.* San Francisco: Jossey-Bass, 1981.

Sechrest, L. B., and Yeaton, W. H. "Magnitudes of Experimental Effects in Social Science Research." *Evaluation Review,* 1982, *6,* 579–600.

Sechrest, L. B., and others. "Some Neglected Problems in Evaluation Research: Strength and Integrity of Treatments." In L. B. Sechrest and others (eds.), *Evaluation Studies Review Annual.* Vol. 4. Newbury Park, Calif.: Sage, 1979.

Shapiro, J. Z. "The Social Costs of Methodological Rigor: A Note on the Problem of Massive Attrition." *Evaluation Review,* 1984a, *8,* 705–712.

Shapiro, J. Z. "Social Justice and Educational Evaluation: Normative Implications of Alternative Criteria for Program Assessment." *Educational Theory,* 1984b, *34,* 137–149.

Sherrill, S. "Toward a Coherent View of Evaluation." *Evaluation Review,* 1984, *8,* 443–466.

Smith, A., Cardillo, J. E., and Choate, R. O. "Age-Based Transition Periods and the Outcome of Mental Health Treatment." *Evaluation and Program Planning,* 1984, *7,* 237–244.

Snowden, L. R. "Treatment Participation and Outcome in a Program for Problem Drinker-Drivers." *Evaluation and Program Planning,* 1984, *7,* 65–71.

Suchman, E. A. *Evaluation Research: Principles and Practices in Public Service and Social Programs.* New York: Russell Sage Foundation, 1967.

Taber, M. A., and Poertner, J. P. "Modeling Service Delivery as a System of Transitions." *Evaluation Review,* 1981, *5,* 549–566.

Trochim, W.M.K. "Framing the Evaluation Question: Some Useful Strategies." Paper presented at the joint meeting of the Evaluation Research Society and Evaluation Network, Chicago, Oct. 1983.

Trochim, W.M.K. "Pattern Matching, Validity, and Conceptualization in Program Evaluation." *Evaluation Review,* 1985, *9,* 575–604.

Trochim, W.M.K. (ed.). *Advances in Quasi-Experimental Design and Analysis.* New Directions for Program Evaluation, no. 31. San Francisco: Jossey-Bass, 1986a.

Trochim, W.M.K. "Editor's Notes." In W.M.K. Trochim (ed.), *Advances in Quasi-Experimental Design and Analysis.* New Directions for Program Evaluation, no. 31. San Francisco: Jossey-Bass, 1986b.

Wang, M.C., and Walberg, H. J. "Evaluating Educational Programs: An Integrative, Causal-Modeling Approach." *Educational Evaluation and Policy Analysis,* 1983, 5, 347–366.

Weinholtz, D., and Friedman, C. P. "Conducting Qualitative Studies Using Theory and Previous Research." *Evaluation and the Health Professions,* 1985, 8, 149–176.

Weiss, C. H. *Evaluation Research: Methods of Assessing Program Effectiveness.* Englewood Cliffs, N.J.: Prentice Hall, 1972.

Wholey, J. S. "Evaluability Assessment: Developing Program Theory." In L. Bickman (ed.), *Using Program Theory in Evaluation.* New Directions for Program Evaluation, no. 33. San Francisco: Jossey-Bass, 1987.

Wilkins, W. "Placebo Problems in Psychotherapy Research: Social-Psychological Alternatives to Chemotherapy Concepts." *American Psychologist,* 1986, 41, 551–556.

Yeaton, W. H. "Proceed With Caution: Using No-Difference Findings to Eliminate Validity Threats." Paper presented at the annual meeting of the American Evaluation Association, Kansas City, Missouri, Oct. 1986.

Yeaton, W. H., and Sechrest, L. B. "Critical Dimensions in the Choice and Maintenance of Successful Treatments: Strength, Integrity, and Effectiveness." *Journal of Consulting and Clinical Psychology,* 1981, 49, 156–167.

Yeaton, W. H., Wortman, P. M., and Langberg, N. "Differential Attrition: Estimating the Effect of Crossovers on the Evaluation of a Medical Technology." *Evaluation Review,* 1983, 7, 831–840.

At the time of publication MARK W. LIPSEY *was a professor in the Department of Human Services, Vanderbilt University, Nashville, Tennessee.*

5

This chapter highlights the continued salience of Weiss's questions about theory-based evaluation, especially given the often simplistic uses of program theory in evaluation.

Theory-Based Evaluation: Reflections Ten Years On

Patricia J. Rogers

Theory-based evaluation has developed significantly since Carol Weiss's chapter was published ten years ago. In 1997 Weiss pointed to theory-based evaluation being mostly used in the areas of health promotion and risk prevention. The use of program theory is now commonplace and Weiss's chapter has been cited in a wide range of program areas, including evaluations of energy conservation (New York State Energy Research and Development Authority, 2006), comprehensive community-based initiatives (Judge and Bauld, 2001), supported housing (Rog and Randolph, 2002), gaming and simulation (Kriz and Hense, 2006), and anticorruption activities (Marra, 2000).

Along with this proliferation of activity has come a proliferation of terminology. Weiss referred to the use of the different terms *program theory* and *logic models* to refer to essentially similar concepts. Now there is an ever-longer list of labels that have been used, not with consistently distinct definitions, including *theory-based, theory-driven, theory-oriented, theory-anchored, theory-of-change, intervention theory, outcomes hierarchies, program theory,* and *program logic.* Despite the use of the term *program,* the method has been used for planning and evaluating interventions ranging from small projects to multisite projects, multiyear strategies and even whole-of-government processes (for example, Public Service Commission, South Africa, 2003).

One of the biggest changes in the use of program theory since 1997 has been its increasing incorporation in program management processes. This phenomenon had occurred earlier in some places and program areas—for

WILEY InterScience® DISCOVER SOMETHING GREAT

NEW DIRECTIONS FOR EVALUATION, no. 114, Summer 2007   © Wiley Periodicals, Inc.
Published online in Wiley InterScience (www.interscience.wiley.com) • DOI: 10.1002/ev.225

example, state and federal governments in Australia had mainstreamed the use of program theory in the 1980s and 1990s (Funnell, 1990), and in the area of international development, many aid agencies had required the use of log frames, a particular type of program theory (*Logical Framework,* 1971). Now many organizations and funders require proposals for projects, programs, and policies to include a logic model or program theory from the beginning in recognition of its value for planning and management, as well as for evaluation. This development has been a primary factor in increasing the number of evaluations that use program theory or logic models of some type and the availability of hard copy and online resources to support the use of program theory.

Despite these developments, Weiss's chapter remains highly relevant because of her warnings about the traps and challenges in using program theory. Many so-called program theory evaluations continue to demonstrate one or more of these limitations, and evaluators would do well either to read or to reread Weiss's discussion of three particular issues, and to examine recent examples that have addressed them.

First, there is the issue of the type of program theory that is used. In her review, Weiss found many evaluations were based on an implementation theory that specifies the activities and some intermediate outcomes, rather than a programmatic theory that specifies the mechanisms of change. Many organizations that claim to have adopted program theory still focus only on implementation theory. They have institutionalized a version involving five or so boxes arranged linearly: inputs, activities, outputs, outcomes, and impacts (again, the terminology is not consistent, and sometimes additional boxes are used for need, context, assumptions, and external factors). These versions, which are often referred to as *program logics* or *logic models* rather than program theories, can be a very good start, particularly for organizations unaccustomed to focusing on outcomes rather than activities, or for programs and policies that are being developed as well as evaluated. However, these simple diagrams fall short of the conceptual summary involved in a *programmatic theory* because they do not examine the causal mechanisms involved in programs and policies—simply using unlabeled arrows to show the links between the components—and do not show the different complementary or alternate causal strands involved in achieving the outcomes. They therefore provide little useful information for replication or improvement. There is nothing wrong with starting with the simple intervention theory; in fact, it is probably difficult to articulate a programmatic theory without at least an implicit implementation theory, but there is a great deal wrong with thinking this is all there is to program theory. Evaluators looking for an example of a program theory with clearly labeled mechanisms could look to Pawson and Tilley's classic realist example of how closed-circuit television in parking lots might work to reduce auto theft through the mechanisms of detection, capture, and removal of thieves; through deterrence; through passive surveillance; and so on (Pawson and Tilley, 1997; Tilley, 2000).

The second issue raised in Weiss's chapter is the quality of the program theory. Weiss found that many of the program theories were based only on practitioners' assumptions and logical reasoning and hence were "simplistic, partial, or even downright wrong." Although it can be useful to articulate practitioners' assumptions about how a program is intended to work, this is often not an adequate program theory for planning and evaluating the program. Unfortunately, many examples of program theory evaluation are still based on poor theories—for example, health promotion programs based solely on the discredited theory that improved knowledge will change attitudes and hence behavior. But how realistic is it to expect an evaluation to include the development of a better program theory or a full-fledged research theory? This is the issue behind Stufflebeam's (2001) trenchant criticism: "There really is not much to recommend theory-based evaluation, since doing it right is usually not feasible and since failed or misrepresented attempts can be counterproductive" (p. 80).

Examples of good practice in program theory evaluation demonstrate that it can be feasible and useful to improve the quality of the theory by better logical analysis of alternative causal explanations, better use of existing research theories, and better use of alternative perspectives on how programs work, including understanding how program clients or intended beneficiaries understand it, and through a process of competitive elaboration and testing against the data. For example, the Centre for Communication Programs at Johns Hopkins University has moved on from using a "Knowledge-Attitudes-Practice" model of behavior change to underpin its evaluations, and now uses the frameworks of "Ideation and Communication for Participatory Development." Murray-Johnson and others (2000–01) compared the utility of four different theories: health belief model, theory of reasoned action, extended parallel process model, and social cognitive theory.

The third issue is how program theory is used in evaluations. In 1997 Weiss observed that many evaluators developed program theory but then did not use it at all to guide the evaluation. This seems less of a problem now, in part because of the widespread practice of developing performance measurement or operationalizing variables on the basis of the program theory. However, the ways program theory are used to guide evaluation are often simplistic. In many cases the evaluation consists only of gathering evidence about each of the components in the logic model, and answering the question "Did this happen?" about each one. Although this can be useful in reporting on the program or policy in terms of a coherent performance story, it does not use the full potential of program theory evaluation, including its ability to address the issue of causal attribution.

There are three possible responses to the challenge of causal attribution. One is to give up the attempt to use program theory evaluation for this purpose, deciding to use it only "to improve, not to prove." Another option is to combine program theory with other methods for causal attribution—for example, Cook (2000) discussed "the false dichotomy" between experimental designs and program theory, and how program theory could be used to design better experiments. Alternatively, a Popperian approach can be taken, and program theory can be used to develop "testable hypotheses," which are then investigated using nonexperimental methods (Pawson and Tilley, 1997; Tilley, 2000). Using the variations among different levels of implementation and different contexts for implementation not as "noise" to be screened out but rather as opportunities to test hypotheses, one can build a stronger case that the program not only contributes to the observed outcomes but also to explaining how. In an international climate of increasing focus on rigorous methods for impact evaluation, this may be the aspect of program theory evaluation most deserving of further development.

References

Cook, T. D. "The False Choice Between Theory-Based Evaluation and Experimentation." In P. J. Rogers, T. A. Hasci, A. Petrosino, and T. A. Huebner (eds.), *Challenges and Opportunities in Program Theory Evaluation.* New Directions in Evaluation, no. 87. San Francisco: Jossey-Bass, 2000.

Funnell, S. "Developments in the New South Wales Approach to Analysing Program Logic." *Proceedings of the Annual Conference of the Australasian Evaluation Society,* 1990, *2,* 247–256.

Judge, K., and Bauld, L. "Strong Theory, Flexible Methods: Evaluating Comprehensive Community-Based Initiatives." *Critical Public Health,* 2001, *11*(1), 19–38.

Kriz, W. C., and Hense, J. U. "Theory-Oriented Evaluation for the Design of and Research in Gaming and Simulation." *Simulation & Gaming,* 2006, *37*(2), 268–283.

"Logical Framework." *An unpublished approach and training materials developed for U.S. Agency for International Development,* 1971.

Marra, M. "How Much Does Evaluation Matter? Some Examples of the Utilization of the Evaluation of the World Bank's Anti-Corruption Activities." *Evaluation,* 2000, *6*(1), 22–36.

Murray-Johnson, L., and others. "Using Health Education Theories to Explain Behaviour Change: A Cross-Country Analysis." *International Quarterly of Community Health Education,* 2000–01, *20*(4), 323–345.

New York State Energy Research and Development Authority. *Quarterly Report to the Department of Public Service. Quarter ending Sept. 30, 2006.* Retrieved Feb. 5, 2007, from http://www.nyserda.org/Energy_Information/SBC/sbcsept2006.pdf.

Pawson, R. D., and Tilley, N. *Realistic Evaluation.* London: Sage, 1997.

Public Service Commission, South Africa. *The PSC's Public Administration Monitoring and Evaluation System: First Consolidated Report.* 2003. Retrieved Feb. 5, 2007, from http://www.pmg.org.za/docs/2003/appendices/031112psc.ppt.

Rog, D. J., and Randolph, F. L. "A Multisite Evaluation of Supported Housing: Lessons Learned from Cross-Site Collaboration." In J. M. Herrell and R. B. Straw (eds.), *Conducting Multiple Site Evaluations in Real-World Settings.* New Directions in Evaluation, no. 94. San Francisco: Jossey-Bass, 2002.

Stufflebeam, D. L. *Evaluation Models.* New Directions for Evaluation, no. 89. San Francisco: Jossey-Bass, 2001.

Tilley, N. *Realistic Evaluation: An Overview.* 2000. Retrieved Feb. 5, 2007, from http://www.danskevalueringsselskab.dk/pdf/Nick%20Tilley.pdf.

Weiss, C. "Theory-Based Evaluation: Past, Present and Future." In D. J. Rog and D. Fournier (eds.), *Progress and Future Directions in Evaluation: Perspectives on Theory, Practice and Methods.* New Directions for Evaluation, no. 76, San Francisco: Jossey-Bass, 1997.

PATRICIA J. ROGERS is associate professor in public sector evaluation and director of CIRCLE (Collaborative Institute for Research, Consulting and Learning) at the Royal Melbourne Institute of Technology, Australia.

Theory-based evaluation examines conditions of program implementation and mechanisms that mediate between processes and outcomes as a means to understand when and how programs work.

Theory-Based Evaluation: Past, Present, and Future

Carol H. Weiss

Theory-based evaluation has surged to attention in recent years. Evaluators are writing about it, and evaluations structured around theory are beginning to appear in numbers in the literature.

The Past

The concept of theory-based evaluation has been around for over twenty-five years. In the spring-summer 1996 issue *Evaluation Practice* published two early papers—an excerpt from my 1972 book *Evaluation Research* and Fitz-Gibbon and Morris (1975)—along with a historical introduction by Blaine Worthen (1996). I have been trying to go back further. In his 1967 book *Evaluative Research*, Edward Suchman referred several times to the notion of programs' theories. Suchman discussed two kinds of reasons for an unsuccessful program: failure of the program to put the intended activities into operation (implementation failure) and failure of the activities to bring about the desired effects (theory failure). My 1972 book offered the first discussion Worthen and I have found of the central idea of basing evaluation on the program's theory. I included a diagram of several alternative theories on which a program of teachers' home visiting might be based. See Figure 5.1. I called the subject a "process model," and I urged that the evaluator collect data on the posited links.

In succeeding years there were a few papers on the subject. Joe Wholey's work on evaluability assessment stressed the need to find out whether the implicit theory underlying a program made sense (Wholey, 1979, 1983). Wholey's idea was that prior to the start of a formal study, the evaluator should analyze the logical reasoning that connected program inputs to

NEW DIRECTIONS FOR EVALUATION, no. 76, Winter 1997 © Jossey-Bass Publishers

Figure 5.1. Theory of a Program of Teacher Home Visits

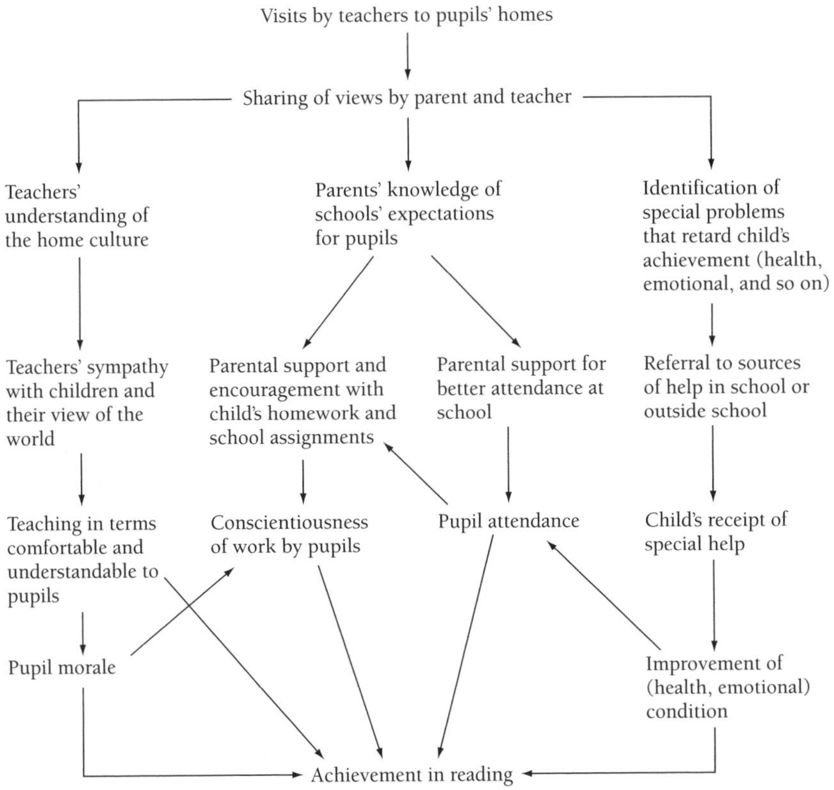

Visits by teachers to pupils' homes

Sharing of views by parent and teacher

Teachers' understanding of the home culture

Parents' knowledge of schools' expectations for pupils

Identification of special problems that retard child's achievement (health, emotional, and so on)

Teachers' sympathy with children and their view of the world

Parental support and encouragement with child's homework and school assignments

Parental support for better attendance at school

Referral to sources of help in school or outside school

Teaching in terms comfortable and understandable to pupils

Conscientiousness of work by pupils

Pupil attendance

Child's receipt of special help

Pupil morale

Improvement of (health, emotional) condition

Achievement in reading

Source: Weiss, 1972, p. 50.

desired outcomes to see whether there was a reasonable likelihood that goals could be achieved.

Huey-Tsyh Chen and Peter Rossi discussed the idea in a series of publications (Chen and Rossi, 1980, 1983, 1987; Chen, 1990, 1994). Their addition to the discussion included the idea that the theory should be a social science theory, not just a series of ad hoc logical premises. Chen (1990) also distinguished between normative theory and causal theory. Normative theory "provides guidance on what goals and outcomes should be pursued or examined" (p. 43), whereas causal theory was the set of assumptions about how the program works. Causal theory is what most of the previous authors and most of the subsequent ones have talked about.

By the late 1980s, program-based evaluation was becoming a popular idea. Although not many examples of theory-based evaluation were yet published, the ideas were becoming increasingly visible. Leonard Bickman edited two issues of New Directions for Program Evaluation (1987 and 1990) that elaborated and advocated the strategy, and Lee Sechrest and A. G. Scott edited one in 1993. Lipsey wrote several articles, one explicating four different versions of program theory. Several articles addressed the subject of how to analyze data that followed the underlying assumptions of a program through time (Judd and Kenny, 1981; Smith, 1990; Marquart, 1990; Trochim, 1985). Dozens of papers appeared.

At the same time, other writers were writing about logic models. Logic models seem to be similar to program theories; at least they are if the word *theory* does not overwhelm us. If we take the word *theory* to mean the professional logic that underlies a program, then the two concepts appear to be much the same.

I wrote a paper on theory-based evaluation in 1995, published in what I thought would be an obscure book, that has received considerable attention (Weiss, 1995). The idea of basing evaluation on programs' theories of change in community-based programs received a warm welcome among evaluators and sponsors of these kinds of programs. One reason seems to be that it promised (or at least hinted at a promise) that theory-based evaluation could strengthen the validity of evaluations when random assignment is impossible, as it is in place-based programming. If the evaluation can show the series of micro-steps that lead from inputs to outcomes, then causal attribution *for all practical purposes* seems to be within reach. Although such an evaluation cannot rule out all the threats to validity we have come to know and love, it has the advantage (if things go well) of showing what processes lead to the outcomes observed; if some of the posited steps are not borne out by the data, then the study can show where the expected sequence of steps breaks down.

The Present

If the past was a period when people developed and elaborated the idea of theory-based evaluation, the present is a time when evaluators are putting the ideas into practice. A graduate student, Jo Birckmayer, and I have done a search for theory-based evaluations in the periodical literature. Mark Lipsey sent me abstracts of studies that his staff coded as "integrated theory" in the evaluation data base he collected some years ago. We are still collecting cases, and I will welcome your papers and articles. We have now inspected about thirty studies that have at least a modicum of theory orientation. This preliminary inspection has given rise to some tentative ideas.

First, quite a number of articles claim that the *programs* are theory-based, and depending on how forgiving our definition of *theory* is, many of them do seem to have a set of coherent ideas providing the basis for intervention. But many of the evaluations do not follow through on that theory; they do not collect data on crucial theoretical constructs. For example, Gottfredson (1987) reports the evaluation of a program to reduce school disorder that is reportedly based on organization development principles.

NEW DIRECTIONS FOR EVALUATION • DOI: 10.1002/ev

However, the evaluation as published does not look at the organizational development aspects. Similarly, Campbell and Ramey (1995) evaluate an early childhood intervention program that is based on theories about enhancement of early cognitive development and the ensuing development of academic confidence, motivation, and success. The evaluation does not track the steps of the program theory.

But a number of evaluations trace the emergence of the stages posited in theory. A few of the theories are simple, what Lipsey and Pollard (1989) would probably call "one-step" theories. Sheard, Marini, Bridges, and Wagner (1976) report on lithium given to aggressive prisoners in a medium-security institution. The evaluation examined the number of violent infractions that they committed. The evaluation thus tested the theory that lithium would reduce violence. The mechanism in this case is the physiological effects that lithium produces in the body. (Actually, the theory is not simple. But the physiological element, the action of lithium in the body, has been investigated by bio-medical researchers and need not form part of the evaluation.)

But some are more complex theories, and the evaluations make valiant efforts to follow them along their course. Cohen and Rice (1995) trace the effects of involving parents in prevention of adolescent substance abuse prevention. They find that parents were difficult to engage, and even when parents attended the program, they did not believe that their children's friends used drugs and so did not monitor their friendships.

Much of the work in theory-based evaluation is going on in the fields of health promotion and risk prevention. Evaluators are using theory-based approaches in programs to reduce smoking, stress, risky sexual behavior, drug abuse, adolescent pregnancy, and similar ills (for example, see Goodman and others, 1996). We have also located a few theory-based studies in mental health and health care (for example, see Bickman, 1983).

Another interesting thing is that evaluators abroad are embracing the approach. When I posted a request for examples of theory-based evaluation on the listserver EVALTALK, I received papers from Rush and Ogborne (1991), in Canada; Torvatn (1995), in Norway; Kelly and Maloney (1992), in Scotland; and Milne (1995), in Australia.

Conditions Conducive to Theory-Based Evaluation. When evaluators adopt a theory-based approach, it is often for one of two reasons. The first is that the evaluator is also the program developer. A program designer, usually an academic, is engaged in a cycle of program development to deal with a particular problem. He or she develops theory, operationalizes the theory in a set of program activities, tests the program and therefore the underlying theory through evaluation, and revises the intervention. Such a cycle has a long and honorable history in several fields of what I would call applied social psychology. Evaluation is part of the ongoing series of activities by which the intervention takes shape. When the work is not that of a single individual but part of the work of an academic center devoted to the design of interventions, evaluation becomes a key feature of both theory development and program modification.

A good example is the work of Sandler and others (1992) at the Program for Prevention Research at Arizona State University who iteratively developed a family bereavement program for youngsters who had lost a parent. Based on prior research and pilot testing, the program aimed to influence four "mediators," hypothesized as implicated in child symptomatology: parental demoralization, parental warmth, discussion of grief, and stable positive events. The evaluation then collected data on the extent to which the program was associated with changes in the four mediators, and went on to study the child's psychosocial symptomatology.

Another condition that promotes a theory-based approach to evaluation is conscientious theory-based development of the program. Health promotion and risk prevention are fields where program planning is well developed: designers tend to spell out their theoretical assumptions in thoughtful detail and build programs on that foundation. Therefore it becomes easy for the evaluator to follow the tracks of theory in the evaluation. Some of the theories are relatively traditional and well established, such as social learning theory. A health promotion program provides knowledge (for example, about methods to break the smoking habit), which leads to a change in motivation and intention (willingness to try to reduce smoking), which leads to a change in practice (cessation of smoking). The change in practice is assumed to lead to the ultimate outcome, which may be reduction in cardiovascular disease. In addition, social-reinforcement theory may call for provision of social supports to encourage and sustain smoking cessation.

Social-cognitive theories of several kinds are prevalent in risk prevention. The operative mechanisms are expected to be change in knowledge, change in attitude, increase in feelings of self-efficacy, higher motivation, mastery of skills, and heightened sense of responsibility, which lead to intentions to change behavior and so on to the desired outcomes. Evaluations follow the anticipated sequence of changes over time.

Program Theory and Implementation Theory. While the subject of theory-based evaluation has been gaining adherents and attention, it has also gained confusion. As is frequently the case with an emerging idea, people have attached their own understandings to the same words. Therefore we have different varieties of recommended evaluation strategies all sailing under the flag of "theory-based evaluation." Figures 5.2–5.5 are diagrams that evaluators have used to explain how their studies have been guided by theory. The diagrams differ in level of specificity, complexity, and type of pictorial display. They also incorporate two different elements of theory, what I will call implementation theory and programmatic theory.

Implementation theory focuses on how the program is carried out. The theoretical assumption it tests is that if the program is conducted as planned, with sufficient quality, intensity, and fidelity to plan, the desired results will be forthcoming. The emphasis is on what Suchman would have

Figure 5.2. Theory of an Antismoking Program

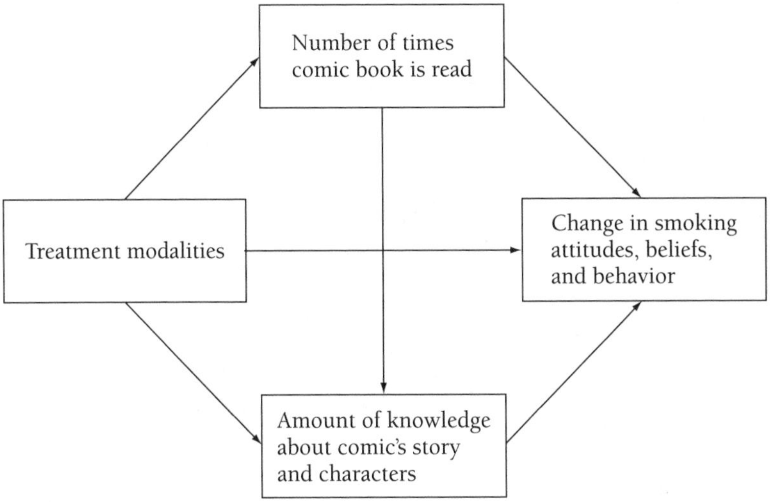

Source: Chen, Quane, Garland, and Marcin, 1988.

called implementation failure/success. Programmatic theory, on the other hand, deals with the *mechanisms* that intervene between the delivery of program service and the occurrence of outcomes of interest. It focuses on participants' responses to program service. The mechanism of change is not the program activities per se but the response that the activities generate. For example, in a contraceptive counseling program, if counseling is associated with reduction in pregnancy, the cause of change might seem to be the counseling. But the mechanism is not the counseling; that is the program activity, the program process. The mechanism might be the knowledge that participants gain from the counseling. Or it might be that the existence of the counseling program helps to overcome cultural taboos against family planning; it might give women confidence and bolster their assertiveness in sexual relationships; it might trigger a shift in the power relations between men and women. These or any of several other cognitive, affective, social responses could be the mechanisms leading to desired outcomes.

Similarly, programs that aim to teach students understanding of other cultures may assume that any good results observed are due to the teaching. But teaching is not the mechanism. The mechanism is what students get from the teaching—knowledge or heightened interest, motivation, even anxiety. An evaluation that attempts to track the theoretical underpinnings of the program has to devise ways to define and measure the psychosocial, physiological, economic, sociological, organizational, or other processes that intervene between exposure to the program and participant outcomes.

Much evaluation that is purportedly theory-based actually examines outcomes in terms of implementation variables. For example, McGraw and

Figure 5.3. Community Prevention Model for Alcohol and Other Drug Abuse

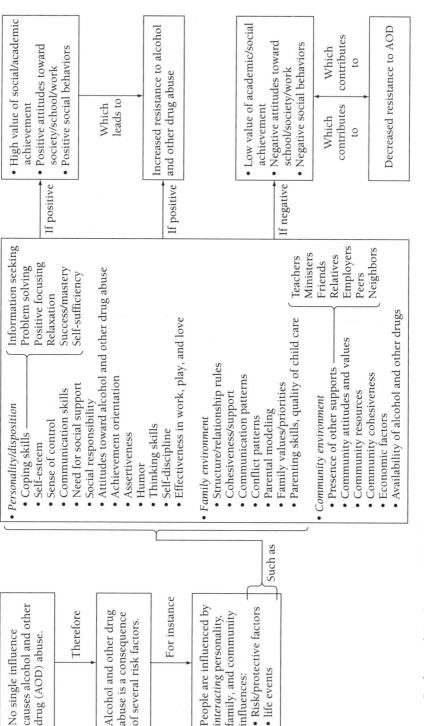

Source: Goodman and Wandersman, 1994, p. 10.

This is a working model. There are other factors, such as genetics.

Figure 5.4. Case Management Theory

Case management activities ⟶ Intermediate outcomes ⟶ Distal outcomes

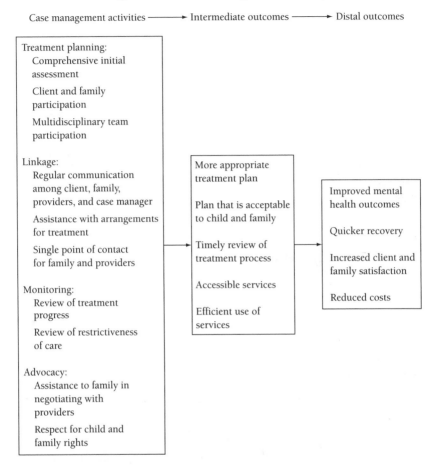

Treatment planning:
  Comprehensive initial
  assessment

  Client and family
  participation

  Multidisciplinary team
  participation

Linkage:
  Regular communication
  among client, family,
  providers, and case manager

  Assistance with arrangements
  for treatment

  Single point of contact
  for family and providers

Monitoring:
  Review of treatment
  progress

  Review of restrictiveness
  of care

Advocacy:
  Assistance to family in
  negotiating with
  providers

  Respect for child and
  family rights

More appropriate
treatment plan

Plan that is acceptable
to child and family

Timely review of
treatment process

Accessible services

Efficient use of
services

Improved mental
health outcomes

Quicker recovery

Increased client and
family satisfaction

Reduced costs

Source: Bryant and Bickman, 1996, p. 123.

others (1996) evaluated a program to change students' dietary knowledge and food choices so as to reduce the risk of cardiovascular disease. The program, called CATCH (Child and Adolescent Trial for Cardiovascular Health), had several components, but the part recently reported related to the classroom component. The outcomes studied were the children's dietary knowledge, self-confidence that they could select better foods, and intentions to eat more wisely. See Figure 5.6. These were analyzed against input variables (mainly student and teacher characteristics) and program processes, such as the extent to which teachers completed the full course of CATCH classroom activities ("dose") and the degree to which teachers modified the activities ("fidelity" to plan). The analysis led to conclusions about

Figure 5.5. Program Theory of an Employment Training Program

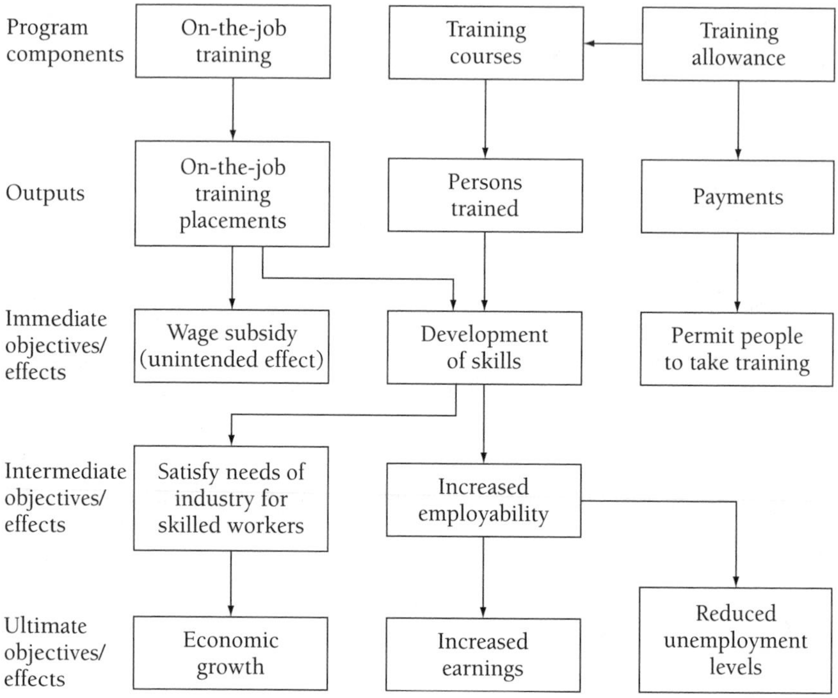

Source: Auditor General of Canada, 1981, p. 14.

the extent to which program activities as defined by CATCH planners led to desired health knowledge and intended behaviors.

This study makes excellent use of process measures in analyzing outcomes. But it does not provide a test of the programmatic theory of the program, at least in this paper. The theory underlying the program is described as "modification of psychosocial factors ... lead[ing] to changes in risk-factor behaviors" (McGraw and others, 1996, p. 292). The evaluation reported does not address the modification of psychosocial factors—that is, it does not inquire into the mechanisms by which change is brought about. Similarly, Pentz and others (1990) do an excellent analysis of the relation between the implementation of a drug abuse prevention program and outcomes for adolescents. The emphasis is strictly on the extent to which implementation variables (such as exposure, adherence, fidelity, and amount of implementation) were associated with outcomes.

The difference between program theory and implementation theory is analogous to the distinction between mediator and moderator variables (Baron and Kenny, 1986). Mediator and moderator variables are both third variables that affect the relation between an independent and a dependent

Figure 5.6. Program Theory Model of the Child and Adolescent Trial for Cardiovascular Health

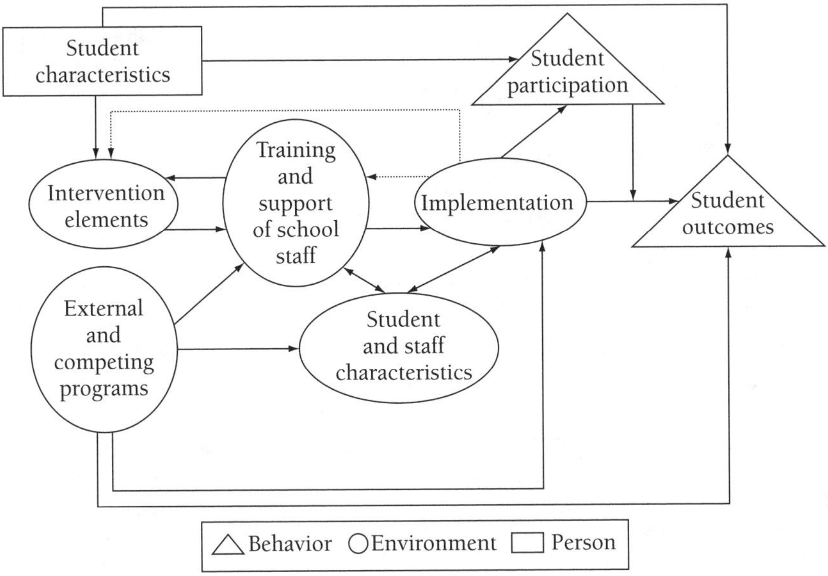

Source: McGraw and others, 1996, p. 294.

variable. The moderator variable is a characteristic, such as gender or frequency of exposure, the subcategories of which have different associations with the outcome variable. Girls do better than boys, or those who attend the program regularly do better than those who attend infrequently. On the other hand, a mediator variable "represents the generative mechanism through which the focal independent variable is able to influence the dependent variable of interest" (Baron and Kenny, 1986, p. 1173). That is, the moderator helps to explain which features of persons or situations have the strongest relationship to the outcome; mediators help to explain how the process works. The concepts are similar to the concepts of implementation theory and programmatic theory.

In most programs both kinds of theories will be implicated. Elsewhere I have used the term *theories of change evaluation* for evaluations that explore both elements.

The Future

Theory-based evaluation is demonstrating its capacity to help readers understand how and why a program works or fails to work. Knowing only outcomes, even if we know them with irreproachable validity, does not tell us enough to inform program improvement or policy revision. Evaluation needs to get inside the black box and to do so systematically.

One of the side benefits of this kind of evaluation is its contribution to wiser program planning even before the evaluation gets under way. When evaluators are involved in the planning phase, they have the opportunity to elicit program designers' own theories about how the program is expected to work. They can help designers to disaggregate the assumptions into the mini-steps that are implied and to confront the leaps of faith and questionable reasoning that are often involved. Evaluators can also offer theories and promising hypotheses based in the social sciences and evidence from prior evaluations that show which kinds of theories hold up in practice. In all these ways, evaluators can become profitably engaged in helping to plan programs that are rooted in better conceived premises.

Challenges lie ahead. One of the immediate needs is for better measures. Through repeated tests, evaluators have made great strides in developing valid measures of outcomes. But measurement of mediating variables is a relatively recent activity in most academic subfields, and evaluators will have to learn how to do it better. Given the large number of variables that are implied in many theories of change, measurement error makes it difficult to identify significant associations among variables—even when they are present. The field needs advances in measurement of mediating mechanisms.

Probably the central need is for better program theories. Evaluators are currently making do with the assumptions that they are able to elicit from program planners and practitioners or with the logical reasoning that they bring to the table. Many of these theories are elementary, simplistic, partial, or even outright wrong. Evaluators need to look to the social sciences, including social psychology, economics, and organization studies, for clues to more valid formulations, and they have to become better versed in theory development themselves. Better theories are important to evaluators as the backbone for their studies. Better theories are even more essential for program designers, so that social interventions have a greater likelihood of achieving the kind of society we hope for in the twenty-first century.

Theory-based evaluation can pursue two different strands in the coming years. One path is to build more detailed program theories, so that evaluations can trace micro-steps of process all along the pathways that lead to program effects. This is like the theory of the teacher home visiting program in Figure 5.1. Each program activity and each participant response is followed along the hypothesized chain of events. There is real promise in this direction, if we iteratively test the linkages between steps and substantially improve our knowledge of how processes work. This kind of evaluation will have much to tell program funders, managers, and practitioners about what works and what does not work under a range of different conditions.

The other path that theory-based evaluation can pursue is to limit the theory to the one or two central assumptions embedded in each program. They should be premises that are significant for program success, common across a range of programs, and particularly problematic. For example, many interventions are now based on the assumption that empowering residents of low-income neighborhoods to help plan social, economic, and educational programs for their community will improve the nature of services. A central premise of these kinds of programs is that residents of the community will plan and allocate resources in ways that are more responsive to need than the professional systems of the past.

Or consider programs to make major alterations in teachers' behavior through staff development programs. The assumption here is that short-term training will be able to modify teaching patterns developed over years of education and professional practice. Another example would be efforts to change such behaviors as low school grades, delinquency, and domestic violence through programs that seek to raise self-esteem and self-confidence. Theory-based evaluation could be directed at investigating the viability of such central theoretical premises.

Evaluations that test such macro-theoretical assumptions will require multiple cases and will be difficult to do. The quest will probably be more appropriate for meta-analysis than for single studies (Cook and others, 1992). Furthermore, they will not hold much interest for funders or practitioners who are wedded to the premise being scrutinized. Professionals who run short-term staff development programs for teachers are not going to be receptive to studies that question whether staff development is a sensible approach to changing teacher behavior.

Still there are audiences who want to know. Program sponsors and funders, whether foundations or government agencies, should have an intense interest in whether the strategy in which they are investing is feasible across a range of conditions. A meta-analysis of evaluations that have measured and examined the same central assumption should have important news to report. It should be able to give insight into the conditions under which these hypotheses hold and the conditions under which they result in shortfalls of varying dimensions. My long-range hope is that evaluation will not only be based on theory but also *contribute* to the cumulation of theoretical knowledge.

Conclusion

Looking at conditions of program implementation that are associated with better outcomes is a real contribution to the improvement of programs. These process/outcome evaluations show which program processes yield positive benefits. Evaluations will provide even more valuable information when they address the mechanisms that mediate between processes and outcomes. Theory-based evaluations attend not only to what programs do but also to how participants respond. Such evaluations are not easy to do, but there are circumstances in which evaluators should proceed in that direction. As a starting point, we need plausible theories. We need to make the maximum use of logical reasoning, practitioner wisdom, prior evaluations, and social science research to generate program theories and then use our collective evaluation work to test them under realistic operating conditions.

References

Auditor General of Canada. *Audit Guide*: Auditing of Procedures for Effectiveness. Ottawa: Office of Auditor General, 1981.

Baron, R. M., and Kenny, D. A. "The Moderator-Mediator Variable Distinction in Social Psychological Research: Conceptual, Strategic, and Statistical Considerations." *Journal of Personality and Social Psychology*, 1986, *51*(6), 1173–1182.

Bickman, L. "The Evaluation of Prevention Programs." *Journal of Social Issues*, 1983, *39*(1), 181–194.

Bickman, L. (ed.). *Using Program Theory in Evaluation*. New Directions for Program Evaluation, no. 33. San Francisco: Jossey-Bass, 1987.

Bickman, L. (ed.). *Advances in Program Theory*. New Directions for Program Evaluation, no. 47. San Francisco: Jossey-Bass, 1990.

Bryant, D. M., and Bickman, L. "Methodology for Evaluating Mental Health Case Management." *Evaluation and Program Planning*, 1996, *19*, 5–16.

Campbell, F. A., and Ramey, C. T. "Cognitive and School Outcomes for High-Risk African-American Students at Middle Adolescence: Positive Effects of Early Intervention." *American Educational Research*, 1995, *32*(4), 743–772.

Chen, H.-T. *Theory-Driven Evaluation: A Comprehensive Perspective*. Newbury Park, Calif.: Sage, 1990.

Chen, H.-T. "Theory-Driven Evaluations: Needs, Difficulties, and Options." *Evaluation Practice*, 1994, *15*, 79–82.

Chen, H.-T., Quane, J., Garland, T. N., and Marcin, P. "Evaluating an Antismoking Program: Diagnostics of Underlying Causal Mechanisms." *Evaluation and the Health Professions*, 1988, *11*(4), 441–464.

Chen, H.-T., and Rossi, P. H. "The Multi-Goal, Theory-Driven Approach to Evaluation: A Model Linking Basic and Applied Social Science." *Social Forces*, 1980, *59*, 106–122.

Chen, H.-T., and Rossi, P. H. "Evaluating with Sense: The Theory-Driven Approach." *Evaluation Review*, 1983, *7*, 283–302.

Chen, H.-T., and Rossi, P. H. "The Theory-Driven Approach to Validity." *Evaluation and Program Planning*, 1987, *10*, 95–103.

Cohen, D. A., and Rice, J. C. "A Parent-Targeted Intervention for Adolescent Substance Use Prevention: Lessons Learned." *Evaluation Review*, 1995, *19*(2), 159–180.

Cook, T. D., Cooper, H., Cordray, D. S., Hartmann, H., Hedges, L. V., Light, R. J., Louis, T. A., and Mosteller, F. *Meta-Analysis for Explanation: A Casebook*. New York: Russell Sage Foundation, 1992.

Fitz-Gibbon, C. T., and Morris, L. L. "Theory-Based Evaluation." *Evaluation Comment*, 1975, *5*(1), 1–4.

Goodman, R. M., and Wandersman, A. "FORECAST: A Formative Approach to Evaluating Community Coalitions and Community-Based Initiatives. *American Journal of Community Psychology*, 1994, special issue, 6–25.

Goodman, R. M., Wandersman, A., Chinman, M., Imm, P., and Morrissey, E. "An Ecological Assessment of Community-Based Interventions for Prevention and Health Promotion: Approaches to Measuring Community Coalitions." *American Journal of Community Psychology*, 1996.

Gottfredson, D. C. "An Evaluation of an Organization Development Approach to Reducing School Disorder." *Evaluation Review*, 1997, *11*(6), 739–763.

Judd, C. M., and Kenny, D. A. "Process Analysis: Estimating Mediation in Treatment Evaluations." *Evaluation Review*, 1981, *5*(5), 602–619.

Kelly, M. P., and Maloney, W. A. "A Behavioural Modelling Approach to Curriculum Development and Evaluation of Health Promotion for Nurses." *Journal of Advanced Nursing*, 1992, *17*, 544–547.

Lipsey, M. W., and Pollard, J. A. "Driving Toward Theory in Program Evaluation: More Models to Choose From." *Evaluation and Program Planning*, 1989, *12*, 317–328.

Marquart, J. M., "A Pattern-Matching Approach to Link Program Theory and Evaluation Data." In L. Bickman (ed.), *Advances in Program Theory*. New Directions for Program Evaluation, no. 47. San Francisco: Jossey-Bass, 1990.

McGraw, S. A., Sellers, D. E., Stone, E. J., Bebchuk, J., Edmundson, E. W., Johnson, C. C., Bachman, K. J., and Luepker, R. V. "Using Process Data to Explain Outcomes: An Illustration from the Child and Adolescent Trial for Cardiovascular Health (CATCH)." *Evaluation Review*, 1996, *20*(3), 291–312.

Milne, C. "Using Program Logic as a Practical Evaluation Tool: Case Studies from an Australian Evaluator." Paper given at First International Evaluation Conference, Vancouver, 1995.

Pentz, M. A., Trebow. E. A., Hansen, W. B., MacKinnon, D. P., Dwyer, J. H., Johnson, C. A., Flay, B. R., Daniels, S., and Cormack, C. "Effects of Program Implementation on Adolescent Drug Use: The Midwestern Prevention Project (MPP)." *Evaluation Review*, 1990, *14*(3), 264–289.

Quane, J. "Back from the Future: Can Evaluation Survive Dissension in the Ranks." Paper prepared for American Evaluation Association meeting, Boston, Nov. 1994.

Rush, B., and Ogborne, A. "Program Logic Models: Expanding Their Role and Structure for Program Planning and Evaluation." *Canadian Journal of Program Evaluation*, 1991, *6*(2), 95–106.

Sandler, I. N., West, S. G., Baca, L., Pillow, D. R., Gersten, J. C., Rogosch, F., Virdin, L., Beak, J., Reynolds, K. D., Kallgren, C., Tein, J-Y., Kriege, G., Cole, E., and Ramirez, R. "Linking Empirically Based Theory and Evaluation: The Family Bereavement Program." *American Journal of Community Psychology*, 1992, *20*(4), 491–521.

Sechrest, L. B., and Scott, A. G. (eds.). "Understanding Causes and Generalizing About Them." New Directions for Program Evaluation, no. 57. San Francisco: Jossey-Bass, 1993.

Sheard, M. H., Marini, J. L., Bridges, C. L., and Wagner, E. "The Effect of Lithium on Impulsive Aggressive Behavior in Man." *American Journal of Psychiatry*, 1976, *133* (12), 1409–1413.

Smith, N. L. "Using Path Analysis to Develop and Evaluate Program Theory." In L. Bickman (ed.), *Advances in Program Theory*. New Directions for Program Evaluation, no. 47. San Francisco: Jossey-Bass, 1990.

Suchman, E. *Evaluative Research*. New York Russell Sage Foundation, 1967.

Torvatn, H. "Chains of Reasoning: An Evaluation Tool." Trondheim, Norway: SINTEF-IFTM paper, 1995.

Trochim, W.M.K. "Pattern Matching, Validity, and Conceptualization in Program Evaluation." *Evaluation Review*, 1985, *9*, 575–604.

Weiss, C. H. *Evaluation Research: Methods for Assessing Program Effectiveness*. Englewood Cliffs N. J.: Prentice Hall, 1972.

Weiss, C. H. "Nothing as Practical as Good Theory." In J. Connell, A. Kubisch, L. B. Schorr, and C. H. Weiss (eds.), *New Approaches to Evaluating Community Initiatives*. New York: Aspen Institute, 1995.

Wholey, J. S. *Evaluation: Promise and Performance*. Washington, D.C.: Urban Institute, 1979.

Wholey, J. S. *Evaluation and Effective Public Management*. Boston: Little, Brown, 1983.

Worthen, B. "Editor's Note: The Origins of Theory-Based Evaluation." *Evaluation Practice*, 1996, *17*(2), 169–171.

At the time of publication CAROL H. WEISS *was a professor of education at the Harvard Graduate School of Education.*

6

In this commentary, a longtime admirer of Cousins and Whitmore discusses why their 1998 article on participatory evaluation made an important contribution to the field.

Making Sense of Participatory Evaluation

Jean A. King

From time to time there comes along an article that helps a field of study make sense of a sizeable body of content. Cousins and Whitmore's following chapter (1998) is one such article. Participatory evaluation was not a new idea in 1998. To a certain extent all program evaluation is participatory—evaluators must, after all, talk to someone when framing a study—but by the mid-1990s articles, chapters, and books that described evaluations where evaluators and staff or program participants engaged in continuing, dynamic interaction throughout a study were commonplace. Indeed, forms of such collaborative inquiry were, as Cousins and Whitmore (1998, p. 5) put it, "emerging at an astounding pace." These forms went by various names—democratic evaluation, empowerment evaluation, developmental evaluation, and action research of differing types, among others—and different people, often from very different conceptual and geographic locales, promoted their value.

The publication of the often-cited Cousins and Whitmore NDE chapter provided two frameworks that, taken together, allowed practitioners and theorists alike to make sense of these many approaches. Documenting its thorough grounding, the chapter has over eighty citations and describes over a dozen different labels for collaborative forms of evaluation practice. The authors had clearly done their homework in gathering the disparate instances of participatory evaluation and took as their task comparing and contrasting those examples to identify similarities and differences. That this

NEW DIRECTIONS FOR EVALUATION, no. 114, Summer 2007   © Wiley Periodicals, Inc.
Published online in Wiley InterScience (www.interscience.wiley.com) • DOI: 10.1002/ev.226

chapter is near the top of those *New Directions for Evaluation* manuscripts most frequently cited speaks to the authors' success.

Cousins and Whitmore's first framework distinguishes between practical participatory evaluation (P-PE) and transformative participatory evaluation (T-PE). The distinction is useful because, on the one hand, it unmistakably differentiates between disparate concepts, but, on the other, points to the commonalities that unite these forms of practice. As its name suggests, practical participatory evaluation "supports organizational and program decision making and problem solving" (1998, p. 6) without necessarily making an explicit commitment to effecting social change. Cousins and Whitmore note that P-PE is a product of United States and Canada practice, where the concepts of responsive evaluation and a stakeholder-based approach had emerged by the early 1970s. By contrast, transformative participatory evaluation, with roots in the developing world (for example, Latin America, India, and Africa), makes an up-front commitment to "democratize social change" (p. 7), "to empower people through participation in the process of constructing and respecting their own knowledge" (p. 8). That distinction made, Cousins and Whitmore then write, "Despite differences that are evident at first blush, T-PE and P-PE have substantial similarities" (p. 10): first, a P-PE project may well empower participants, while a T-PE project can also have practical value, and, second, creating data from the practitioners' perspectives (what Cousins and Whitmore call "valid local data") is centrally important to each approach.

The chapter's second framework provides a set of "process dimensions" for analyzing collaborative inquiry. Using the graphic of a three-dimensional plus sign, Cousins and Whitmore propose three dimensions for distinguishing forms of participatory inquiry: (1) control of the evaluation process (from research-controlled to practitioner-controlled); (2) stakeholder selection for participation (from primary users to "all legitimate groups"); and (3) depth of participation (from mere consultation to "deep participation"). Analysis can then identify specific participatory processes by assigning numbers to the dimensions (1, 2, and 3) and letters to the ends of the continua (a and b). Transformative participatory evaluation, for example, is a1-b1-c2—practitioner control (a1) of deep participation (c2) by primary users (b1). Cousins and Whitmore use their process dimensions to contrast ten forms of "systematic inquiry," including the two types of participatory evaluation, other forms of collaborative evaluation, and other forms of collaborative inquiry. The analysis is presented in a summary table (1998, pp. 12–13).

Some of the results are not surprising. For example, emancipatory (participatory) action research and the cooperative inquiry as described by Heron (1981) and Reason (1994) share the same coordinates as transformative participatory evaluation. Others are more provocative. Stakeholder-based evaluation "bears the least resemblance to either form of PE" (Cousins and Whitmore, 1998, p. 14) because, despite its name, it involves researcher-controlled (a2) consultation (a1) with all legitimate groups (b2), moving it far from the extensive interaction common to participatory approaches. And empowerment evaluation as operationalized by Fetterman (1994) and Fetterman, Kaftarian, and Wandersman (1996) "is in some respects enigmatic" (Cousins and Whitmore, 1998, p. 15): "This analysis suggests quite strongly that empowerment evaluation, in practice, tends to be best conceptualized as a form of P-PE [rather than T-PE]" (p. 16). Regardless of the outcomes of Cousins and Whitmore's analysis, the process dimensions create a framework for analyzing any evaluation approach that purports to be participatory and for grouping it with similar approaches that came before, a helpful contribution to a field known for proliferating different names for new approaches.

Cousins and Whitmore end their chapter by posing seven questions that they say are neither new nor "unique to PE as an approach to collaborative inquiry" (1998, p.18), but deserving of consideration. The seven topics are power and its ramifications, ethics, participant selection, technical quality, cross-cultural issues, training, and conditions that facilitate PE. This list touches on issues that continue to be critical to the practice of participatory evaluation, whether practical or transformative. The inclusion of cross-cultural concerns, for example, "How can cultural, language, or racial barriers be addressed?" (p. 18), documents the elevation of this topic as an issue essential to high-quality practice.

The content of Cousins and Whitmore has implications for both practice and theory that have continued to be widely discussed in the nearly ten years since its publication. The importance of this chapter, finally, comes from its two frameworks, which allow practitioners and theorists alike to place their practice in a participatory context, and from the set of questions, which encourages them to think purposefully about improvement. These frameworks are analytical but also generative because they raise questions about how to conduct or study participatory evaluation. Forms of practical participatory evaluation have grown under labels like organizational learning, process use, developmental evaluation, and data-driven decision making. Transformative participatory evaluation practice now encompasses approaches like deliberative democratic evaluation, inclusive evaluation, and values-driven evaluation, all of which focus on a constructivist epistemology and social betterment as evaluation's ultimate goal. Thanks to Brad Cousins and Bessa Whitmore, the field has a way to understand and capture the distinctions among these many approaches.

References

Cousins, J. B., and Whitmore, E. "Framing Participatory Evaluation." In E. Whitmore (ed.), *Understanding and Practicing Participatory Evaluation.* New Directions for Evaluation, no. 80. San Francisco, 1998.

Fetterman, D. M. "Empowerment Evaluation," *Evaluation Practice,* 1994, *15*(1), 1–15.

Fetterman, D. M., Kaftarian, S. J., and Wandersman, A. *Empowerment Evaluation: Knowledge and Tools for Self-Assessment and Accountability*. Thousand Oaks, Calif.: Sage, 1996.

Heron, J. "Validity in Co-operative Inquiry." In P. Reason (ed.), *Human Inquiry in Action*. London: Sage, 1981.

Reason, P. "Three Approaches to Participative Inquiry." In N. K. Denzin and Y. S. Lincoln (eds.), *Handbook of Qualitative Research*. Thousand Oaks, Calif.: Sage, 1994.

JEAN A. KING *is the coordinator of evaluation studies for the Department of Educational Policy and Administration at the University of Minnesota and a longtime practitioner of participatory evaluation.*

NEW DIRECTIONS FOR EVALUATION • DOI: 10.1002/ev

This chapter posits two principal streams of participatory evaluation, practical participatory evaluation and transformative participatory evaluation, and compares them on a set of dimensions relating to control, level, and range of participation. The authors then situate them among other forms of collaborative evaluations.

Framing Participatory Evaluation

J. Bradley Cousins, Elizabeth Whitmore

Forms and applications of collaborative research and inquiry are emerging at an astounding pace. For example, a bibliography of published works on participatory research in the health-promotion sector listed close to five hundred titles (Green and others, 1995), with some items dating back as early as the late 1940s. The vast majority, however, have surfaced since the mid-1970s. In the evaluation field, one label that is being used with increasing frequency as a descriptor of collaborative work is *participatory evaluation* (PE). The term, however, is used quite differently by different people. For some it implies a practical approach to broadening decision making and problem solving through systematic inquiry; for others, reallocating power in the production of knowledge and promoting social change are the root issues.

The purpose of this chapter is to explore the meanings of PE through the identification and explication of key conceptual dimensions. We are persuaded of the existence of two principal streams of participatory evaluation, streams that loosely correspond to pragmatic and emancipatory functions. After describing these streams, we present a framework for differentiating among forms of collaborative inquiry and apply it as a way to (1) compare the two streams of participatory evaluation and (2) situate them among other forms of collaborative evaluation and collaborative inquiry. We conclude with a set of questions confronted by those with an interest in participatory evaluation.

Two Streams

Participatory evaluation implies that, when doing an evaluation, researchers, facilitators, or professional evaluators collaborate in some way with individuals, groups, or communities who have a decided stake in the program, development project, or other entity being evaluated. In the North American literature stakeholders are typically defined as those with a vested interest in the focus for evaluation (Mark and Shotland, 1985), although some authors prefer a finer distinction (Alkin, 1991). Stakeholders might be program sponsors, managers, developers, and implementors. Members of special-interest groups and program beneficiaries also have an identifiable stake in the program. In the evaluation literature arising in international- and community-development contexts, the term *stakeholder* is not explicitly used, nor is evaluation typically bounded by the parameters of a specific program. Nevertheless, consideration is given to the perspectives of various groups or communities within these development contexts, particularly as related to their involvement and participation. It can be assumed that many members of these groups have minimal experience with and training in evaluation or formal methods of applied systematic inquiry. Although the general principle of collaboration between evaluators and nonevaluators applies to virtually all forms of participatory evaluation, distinguishing features associated with goals and purposes and with historical and ideological roots help to delineate two identifiable approaches.

Garaway (1995) acknowledges that most applications of participatory evaluation combine rationales and attempt to integrate multiple purposes in a single evaluation project. Nonetheless, she differentiates between two specific rationales. Pursley (1996) makes similar arguments. Both authors subscribe to the view that one form of participatory evaluation is practical and supports program or organizational decision making and problem solving. We term this approach *practical participatory evaluation* (P-PE). A second rationale has as its foundation principles of emancipation and social justice; it seeks to empower members of community groups who are less powerful than or are otherwise oppressed by dominating groups. Our term for this approach is *transformative participatory evaluation* (T-PE).

Practical Participatory Evaluation (P-PE). Practical participatory evaluation has arisen primarily in the United States and Canada. It has as its central function the fostering of evaluation use, with the implicit assumption that evaluation is geared toward program, policy, or organizational decision making. The core premise of P-PE is that stakeholder participation in evaluation will enhance evaluation relevance, ownership, and thus utilization. The utilization construct has been traditionally conceptualized in terms of three types of effects or uses of evaluation findings: (1) instrumental, the provision of support for discrete decisions; (2) conceptual, as in an educative or learning function; and (3) symbolic, the persuasive or political use of evaluation to reaffirm decisions already made or to further a particular agenda (Leviton and Hughes, 1981; King, 1988; Weiss, 1972, 1979). Typically, impact is conceptualized in terms of effects on an undifferentiated group of "users" or "decision makers."

Shulha and Cousins (1996) describe several developments in the evaluation-utilization field that have emerged since the mid-1980s. First, many researchers have observed that utilization is often associated at least as much with the process of doing the evaluation as with the findings themselves (for example, Cousins, Donohue, and Bloom, 1996; Greene, 1988; Patton, 1997b; Preskill, 1994; Whitmore, 1991). Second, several researchers advocate an expanded role for utilization-oriented evaluators that incorporates elements of planned-change agentry (Mathison, 1994; Preskill, 1994; Owen and Lambert, 1995; Whitmore, 1988). Third, conceptions of utilization and evaluation impact are being extended beyond the particular program or target for evaluation to include organizational learning and change (Cousins and Earl, 1995; Jenlink, 1994; Owen and Lambert, 1995; Torres, Preskill, and Piontek, 1996). Each of these developments represents part of an integrated rationale for P-PE.

Building on principles of "sustained interactivity" between evaluators and program practitioners (Huberman and Cox, 1990) and on the observation that increased stakeholder involvement in evaluation renders the process responsive to user needs, several researchers have implemented and studied various forms of P-PE. Greene (1988) reported a study of an evaluation process that fairly closely resembled the conventional stakeholder-based approach (Bryk, 1983). Here evaluators assume responsibility for carrying out technical evaluation tasks, and stakeholders are involved predominantly in definition of the evaluation problem, scope-setting activities, and, later, interpreting data emerging from the study. Ayers (1987) described a similar model—the "stakeholder-collaborative approach," where stakeholders participate as partners, share joint responsibility for the study, and are primarily accountable for its results. A similar form of collaboration was detailed by King (1995). Cousins and Earl (1992, 1995) outlined an approach they labeled *participatory evaluation*, which built on the conventional stakeholder model by advocating joint ownership and control of technical evaluation decision making, a more penetrating role for stakeholders, and restriction of participation to stakeholders most closely connected with the program.

Despite the identification of countervailing influences, such as micropolitical processes or the lack of organizational or administrative support for the evaluation (Cousins and Earl, 1995; King, 1995), each of the foregoing researchers provide empirical evidence for the potent influence of these forms of P-PE in enhancing the utilization of both evaluation findings and process. Moreover, it has been demonstrated that under appropriate conditions participation by stakeholders can enhance utilization without compromising technical quality or credibility (Cousins, 1996; Greene, 1988). Process effects include influences on affective dimensions (for example, feelings of self-worth and empowerment), the development of an appreciation and acceptance of evaluation, and the development of skills associated with the act of systematic inquiry (Whitmore, 1988). Some of these process effects overlap with those emerging from T-PE processes described below.

Transformative Participatory Evaluation (T-PE). Transformative participatory evaluation invokes participatory principles and actions in order to democratize social change; it has quite different ideological and historical roots from P-PE. Most of the literature on T-PE relates primarily to participatory research and, later, to participatory action research, although PE is addressed directly at times. The background and principles are shared by PE. Based on a more radical ideology than P-PE, T-PE emerged in the early 1970s, primarily but not exclusively in the developing world—notably Latin America (Fals-Borda, 1980), India (Fernandes and Tandon, 1981; Tandon, 1981), and Africa (Kassam and Mustafa, 1982)—in part as a reaction to positivist models of inquiry that were seen as exploitive and detached from urgent social and economic problems. The work of these researchers was framed explicitly within contexts of power and transformation (Hall, 1992). An international participatory-research network was established in the 1970s, with headquarters in India, and the first of a series of major international seminars was held in Tanzania in 1979 (Kassam and Mustafa, 1982). These initiatives sparked a period of intense theoretical and practical activity in participatory research and evaluation. Although T-PE is now spreading to the university sector, it is deeply rooted in community and international development, adult education, and, more recently, the women's movement.

Dependency theorists saw conventional research methods as leading to cultural dependency and as denying the knowledge-creating abilities of ordinary people (Hall, 1977). The work of the Brazilian adult educator Paolo Freire has been pivotal in establishing the philosophical foundations of T-PE (1970, 1982). Other influences include some of the early work of Karl Marx and Friedrich Engels; Antonio Gramsci's notions of the "organic intellectual," hegemony, and civil society; Jürgen Habermas; T. W. Adorno; and the critical theorists (Hall, 1992; Maguire, 1987). Although the early roots of T-PE took hold outside North America, important work in this area has been done through the Highlander Research and Education Center in Tennessee (Gaventa, 1980, 1981, 1988), and the Toronto-based Participatory Research Group (Hall, 1977).

Several key concepts underpin T-PE. Most fundamental is the issue of who creates and controls the production of knowledge. One important aim of T-PE is to empower people through participation in the process of constructing and respecting their own knowledge (based on Freire's notion of "conscientization") and through their understanding of the connections among knowledge, power, and control (Fals-Borda and Anisur-Rahman, 1991; Tandon, 1981). No contradiction is seen between collective empowerment and deepening social knowledge (Hall, 1992); popular knowledge is assumed to be as valid and useful as scientific knowledge. A second key concept relates to process. How is the evaluation conducted? The distance between researcher and researched is broken down; all participants are contributors working collectively. Initiating and sustaining genuine dialogue among actors leads to a deep level of understanding and mutual respect (Gaventa, 1993; Whitmore, 1991, 1994). A third concept, critical reflection, requires participants to question, to doubt, and to consider a broad range of social factors, including their own biases and assumptions (Comstock and Fox, 1993).

Participatory research has been described as a three-pronged activity involving investigation, education, and action (Hall, 1981). Likewise, T-PE, by helping create conditions where participants can empower themselves, focuses not only on data collection, analysis, and dissemination but also on learning inherent in the process and on any actions that may result. T-PE has as its primary function the empowerment of individuals or groups. Rappaport defined empowerment as "both a psychological sense of personal control or influence and concern with actual social influence, political power and legal rights" (1987, p. 121, cited in Perry and Backus, 1995). In this approach, evaluation processes and products are used to transform power relations and to promote social action and change. Evaluation is conceived as a developmental process where, through the involvement of less powerful stakeholders in investigation, reflection, negotiation, decision making, and knowledge creations, individual participants and power dynamics in the sociocultural milieu are changed (Pursley, 1996).

Brunner and Guzman (1989) characterize T-PE as an emergent form of evaluation that takes the interests, preoccupations, aspirations, and priorities of the so-called target populations and their facilitators into account. "The social groups, together with their facilitators, decide when an evaluation should take place, what should be evaluated, how the evaluation should be carried out, and what should be done with the result" (pp. 10–11). In this sense, PE is an "educational process through which social groups produce action-oriented knowledge about their reality, clarify and articulate their norms and values, and reach consensus about further action" (p. 11). Initially, the evaluation team (comprising all participants in the project) may be fairly dependent on professional evaluators and facilitators for training, but they soon become more sophisticated. Ultimately, they are responsible for organizing and implementing the evaluation, disseminating its results, systematizing group interpretations, coordinating group decision making about project change, and ensuring that action is taken.

Much PE literature has emerged from the international- and community-development fields (Campos, 1990; Coupal, 1995; Feuerstein, 1988; Forss, 1989; Freedman, 1994; Jackson and Kassam, in press; Lackey, Peterson, and Pine, 1981; Rugh, 1994). As a result, a number of PE handbooks and assorted practical materials for grassroots groups have been published (African Development Foundation, n.d.; Ellis, Reid, and Barnsley, 1990; Feuerstein, 1986; United Nations Development Program, 1997).

Comparison of Approaches. Although these two streams of participatory evaluation are distinguishable from one another on the basis of their central goals, functions, and historical and ideological roots, there is clearly an overlap between the two. For example, it is difficult to imagine that participation in a P-PE project that led to an understanding of program functions and processes and to the development of skills in systematic inquiry would not, concomitantly, empower that program practitioner (or group). Equally, a T-PE project that led individuals to take control of their own development-project functions or circumstances would probably also prove to be of considerable practical value in project development and implementation.

Apart from the overlap among central and secondary goals for PE, both streams overlap with yet a third rationale for collaborative inquiry. Identified by Levin (1993) as epistemological or philosophical in nature (or both), this argument posits that research knowledge and evaluation data are valid only when informed by practitioner perspectives. Although Guba and Lincoln (1989) argue this point vehemently, their approach to evaluation is not necessarily participatory, given the dominant role played by the evaluator in immersing herself or himself in the local context and constructing meaning from that perspective. Yet one can easily imagine that the development of valid local knowledge, based on shared understanding and the joint construction of meaning, would be integral to both forms of PE.

Thus, we conclude that P-PE and T-PE differ in their primary functions—practical problem solving versus empowerment—and ideological and historical roots but overlap in their secondary functions and in other areas. Despite differences that are evident at first blush, T-PE and P-PE have substantial similarities.

Differentiating Process Dimensions of Collaborative Inquiry

We propose three distinguishing characteristics of PE. The first is *control of the evaluation process,* ranging from control of decisions being completely in the hands of the researcher to control being exerted entirely by practitioners. Control here relates particularly to technical decisions—those regarding evaluation processes and conduct—as opposed to decisions about whether and when to initiate evaluation. The second characteristic is *stakeholder selection* for participation, ranging from restriction to primary users to inclusion of all legitimate groups. The third characteristic is *depth of participation,* from consultation (with no decision-making control or responsibility) to deep participation (involvement in all aspects of an evaluation from design, data collection, analysis, and reporting to decisions about dissemination of results and use). A PE process can be located somewhere on these continua, depending on who controls the process and on who participates and how much. Shulha and Cousins (1995) observed that these distinguishing features correspond to basic dimensions or continua along which any given collaborative research project might be located. Cousins, Donohue, and Bloom (1996) made a similar case for differentiating among various forms of collaborative evaluation and between collaborative and noncollaborative evaluation.

If we accept that these three dimensions are useful for differentiating collaborative approaches to systematic inquiry, we might also consider that they may be independent of one another. Decisions about who participates, to what extent they participate, and who controls technical decision making can, in theory, be made independently of each other. Empirically such independence seems unlikely, but heuristically this distinction is a useful one. Figure 6.1 represents the characteristics in three-dimensional space. This device may be used to consider the collaborative processes associated with a variety of genres of collaborative and even noncollaborative inquiry. Any given example may be considered in terms of its location on each of the dimensions, thereby yielding its geometric coordinate location. We can now integrate this framework with our prior discussion of goals and functions in order to answer the following questions:

- How do P-PE and T-PE differ from one another?
- How do forms of PE differ from other forms of collaborative evaluation?
- How do forms of PE differ from other forms of collaborative inquiry?

As an aid to making such determinations, a wide variety of approaches to collaborative inquiry and evaluation are described in Table 6.1 and considered below. (Only representative forms of the various categories in Table 6.1 are discussed.)

How Do P-PE and T-PE Differ? Differences in the goals and functions and in the historical roots of these two streams of PE are explicated above

Figure 6.1. Dimensions of Form in Collaborative Inquiry

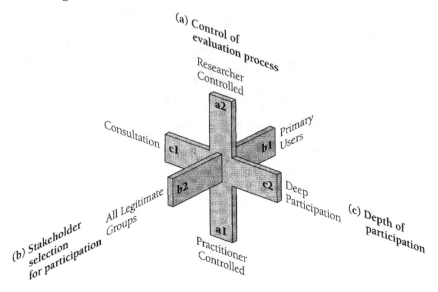

Table 6.1. Forms of Systematic Inquiry by Goals and Process Dimensions

Label	Principal Author(s)	Primary Technical Goal/Functions	Dimensions of Process in Collaborative Inquiry			Location in Figure 6.1
			Control of Decision Making	Selection for Participation	Depth of Participation	
A. Participatory Evaluation						
Practical Participatory Evaluation (P-PE)	Cousins and Earl (1992, 1995); Ayers (1987)	Practical: support for program decision making and problem solving; evaluation utilization	Balanced: evaluator and participants in partnership	Primary Users: program sponsors, managers, developers, implementors	Extensive: participation in all phases of the evaluation	a1–a2 b1 c2
Transformative Participatory Evaluation (T-PE)	Tandon and Fernandes (1982, 1984); Fals-Borda (1980); Gaventa (1993)	Political: empowerment, emancipation, social justice	Balanced: partnership but ultimate decision-making control by participants	All legitimate groups: especially program or project beneficiaries	Extensive: participation in all phases of the evaluation	a1 b2 c2
B. Other Forms of Collaborative Evaluation						
Stakeholder-Based Evaluation	Bryk (1983); Mark and Shotland (1985)	Practical: evaluation utilization; some emphasis on political aspects of evaluation	Evaluator: coordinator of activities and technical aspects of the evaluation	All legitimate groups: representation is key to offsetting ill effects of program micropolitics	Limited: stakeholders consulted at planning and interpretation phases	a2 b2 c1
School-Based Evaluation	Nevo (1993, 1994); Alvik (1995)	Practical: support for program decision making and problem solving	Balanced: evaluator trains school-based personnel who do their own inquiry	Primary users: school-based personnel, mostly program implementors	Extensive: participation in all phases of the evaluation	a1–a2 b2 c2
Democratic Evaluation	MacDonald (1976); McTaggart (1991b)	Political: legitimate use of evaluation in pluralistic society	Balanced: evaluator and participants work in partnership	All legitimate groups: representation among participants is pivotal	Moderate: stakeholders control interpretation and reporting	a1–a2 b2 c1–c2

Developmental Evaluation	Patton (1994)	Practical: program improvement; evaluation utilization	Balanced: evaluator and participants work in partnership	Primary users: mostly program developers and implementors	Substantial: ongoing involvement and participation	a1–a2 b1 c2
Empowerment Evaluation	Fetterman (1994, 1995)	Political: empowerment, illumination, self-determination	Participants: almost complete control, facilitated by evaluator	Primary users: usually key program personnel; sometimes wider groups included	Extensive: participation in all phases of the evaluation	a1 b1 c1
C. Other Forms of Collaborative Inquiry						
Participatory Action Research	Whyte (1991); Argyris and Schön (1991)	Practical/philosophical: improve practice while simultaneously advancing scientific knowledge	Balanced: researcher and practitioner as coparticipants in research	Primary users: most often program implementors, although can be open to beneficiaries and others	Extensive: participation in all aspects of the research	a1–a2 b1 c2
Emancipatory (Participatory) Action Research	Carr and Kemmis (1992); McTaggart (1991a)	Political: empowerment, emancipation, amelioration of social conditions	Practitioner: exclusive control; researcher as resource person	Unspecified: most often stakeholders who are disenfranchised or in some way marginalized by the system	Extensive: participation in all aspects of the research	a1 b2 c2
Cooperative Inquiry	Heron (1981); Reason (1994); Reason and Heron (1986)	Philosophical: root propositional research knowledge about people in their experiental and practical knowledge	Practitioner: participants are both co-researchers and co-subjects with full reciprocity	Unspecified: most often participants are members of an inquiry group with all of the problems of inclusion, influence, and intimacy	Extensive: participation in all aspects of the research	a1 b2 c2

and require no further elaboration here. After examining the dimensions of process, one might conclude that these approaches are quite similar, with the exception of who participates in the evaluation exercise. In the Cousins and Earl model (1992, 1995), the emphasis is on fostering program decision making and organizational problem solving, and evaluators tend to work in partnership with potential users who have the clout to do something with the evaluation findings or emergent recommendations. Although this approach accommodates participation by others, potential users' ownership of and inclination to use evaluation data will be limited without the involvement of key personnel. Indeed, such unsatisfactory outcomes have been demonstrated empirically (Cousins, 1995; King, 1995; Lafleur, 1995). Part of the rationale for limiting participation to stakeholders closely associated with program support and management is that the evaluation stands a better chance of meeting the program and organizational decision makers' time lines and need for information. Although the evaluator acts on behalf of the primary users by guarding against the intrusion of self-serving interests (mostly by holding program practitioner participants to the data and findings), the model is not as useful when there is a disagreement or lack of consensus among stakeholder groups about program goals or intentions. In such cases, conflict among competing interest groups needs to be resolved, and if stakeholder participation is limited to primary decision makers, the evaluation is likely to be seen as illegitimate and biased. For evaluators finding themselves in situations of this sort, the prudence of their acting in a conflict-resolution mode or their ability to resist being co-opted by powerful stakeholders (or both) raises questions.

However, T-PE more generally than P-PE involves participation by stakeholders, especially beneficiaries, members of the program, or the development project's target population. In this sense, power issues are more directly addressed. Of course, program beneficiaries are the population that T-PE is intended to serve through fostering empowerment and illuminating key social and program issues. Although evaluators and facilitators may have direct roles in training practitioners, dependence on such professionals diminishes as time passes and local experience is acquired. This may also be the case for P-PE. Cousins and Earl (1995) note that dealing with organizational constraints and integrating evaluation and participation into the culture of organizations are formidable tasks, destined to unfold over several repetitions and protracted periods of time.

Both forms of PE share the intention of involving stakeholders and community members in all aspects of the evaluation project, including the highly technical ones. For practical and logistical reasons, Cousins and Earl (1995) question the value and viability of engaging practitioners in highly technical activities. In some contexts, however, community members may be better than evaluators at some technical tasks (Chambers, 1997; Gaventa, 1993). In either approach, the assumption that mastery of such technical tasks is a form of empowerment remains intact.

How Do Forms of PE Differ from Other Forms of Collaborative Evaluation? In Panel B of Table 6.1, five examples of alternative forms of collaborative evaluation are described. Perhaps the best known of these—stakeholder-based evaluation—bears the least resemblance to either form of PE. This may seem somewhat surprising, particularly in view of the fact that P-PE was conceived to be an extension of the stakeholder-based model (Cousins and Earl, 1992). Stakeholder-based evaluation has similar goals to P-PE but is perhaps better suited to situations where widespread agreement among stakeholder groups about program goals is lacking. By involving all legitimate groups in the process, the evaluator is able to pit those who subscribe to different value positions against one another while maintaining a generally neutral stance. In working toward consensus building, the evaluative process becomes more useful to a wider audience than would be the case if only one, or some, stakeholder groups were included. By controlling the technical decision making and by operating in the role of mediator or facilitator, the evaluator is better able to protect herself or himself from being co-opted. Whereas P-PE is best suited to formative evaluation problems (Ayers, 1987; Cousins and Earl, 1992, 1995), stakeholder evaluation is a viable approach to decision-oriented or decidedly summative evaluation questions. However, stakeholder-based evaluation differs from T-PE by virtue of its practical goals, evaluator control, and limited stakeholder participation in a wide range of evaluation activities. Although most authors describe its functions in pragmatic terms, Mark and Shotland (1985) suggest that emancipatory and representativeness rationales underlie the implementation of stakeholder-based evaluation. However, in a survey of evaluators, Cousins, Donohue, and Bloom (1996) observed that much of the collaborative evaluation practice in North America is aligned with the stakeholder-based model. Most of the reports examined suggest that practical decision making and problem solving were the forces driving the model's implementation.

Of the four alternatives to stakeholder-based evaluation listed in Table 6.1 (Panel B), two are more closely aligned with the more practical stream of PE, while the remaining two tend to resemble the more political stream. First, both democratic and empowerment evaluation are similar to T-PE. Democratic evaluation is intended to maximize the utility of evaluation in a pluralistic society (MacDonald, 1976). In this respect it is similar to stakeholder-based evaluation. Evaluators and participants work in partnership, sharing the work and the decisions. The evaluation is rendered democratic "by giving participants considerable control over the interpretation and release of information" (McTaggart, p. 10, 1991b). Stakeholders include all legitimate groups, a key point. To that end, representativeness among legitimate stakeholder groups and a cooperative working relationship between evaluators and stakeholders are pivotal.

Although similarly targeted on political goals, empowerment evaluation (Fetterman, 1994, 1995) holds as key objectives the empowerment of individuals and groups, the illumination of issues of concern to them, and the development of a basic sense of self-determination. Because these goals are manifestly emancipatory, empowerment evaluation is more closely linked to T-PE than to P-PE. But this approach, as described by Fetterman (1994; Fetterman, Kaftarian, and Wandersman, 1996), is in some respects enigmatic. In one instance, the evaluator acts exclusively in a facilitation mode, helping to support program or project personnel in their efforts to become self-sufficient. In another instance, the evaluator is "morally compelled" to assume an advocacy role for groups with less power and voice. Variation between these two examples of empowerment evaluation, both in the locus of control and in the meaning of participation, is considerable. The approach also differs from T-PE inasmuch as evaluators tend to work with those closely associated with the project being evaluated rather than with a wider array of stakeholders. Finally, Patton (1997a) conducted a careful analysis of the examples of empowerment evaluation compiled by Fetterman, Kaftarian, and Wandersman (1996) and concluded that many of these cases are exemplars of "participatory, collaborative, stakeholder-involving, and even utilization-focussed evaluations, and really do not meet the criteria for empowerment" (p. 149). This analysis suggests quite strongly that empowerment evaluation, in practice, tends to be best conceptualized as a form of P-PE.

Similarities with P-PE are apparent in descriptions of school-based evaluation and developmental evaluation. Nevo (1993, 1994) advocates developing "evaluation-mindedness" in schools through training, support, and school-based mechanisms for evaluation. Such mechanisms provide a basis for dialogue between school staff and those outside the school who request accountability, and although they are conducted internally and exclusively by school staff, they could feed into subsequent external, summative evaluations. School-based evaluation's focus on integrating evaluation into the organizational culture of schools and its focus on stakeholders closely linked to the program and their involvement in all phases of the evaluation are features that match those of P-PE. In developmental evaluation, however, evaluators work closely with program developers by helping them integrate evaluation into the development phase of programming (Patton, 1994, 1997b). In this model the evaluator works in partnership with developers, but stakeholder participation in the evaluation is comparatively limited. In a sense stakeholders represent the development function of the partnership, and although they are fully appraised of and able to shape the evaluation, their direct participation remains peripheral. This approach fairly closely resembles P-PE, with the exception of the depth of participation.

How Do Forms of PE Differ from Other Forms of Collaborative Inquiry? Although evaluation is directly linked to judgments about the merit and worth of a particular program, project, or innovation and thus provides a systematic basis to support decision making, forms of systematic inquiry designed for other purposes may also be carried out on a collaborative basis and are therefore worth comparing and contrasting with PE. Indeed, such comparisons have been made before (Huberman, 1995; King, 1995). In Table 6.1, Panel C, three alternative forms of participative inquiry are described. One of these, a North American adaptation of participatory action research (PAR), bears some resemblance to P-PE; another, emancipatory action research, is more closely related to T-PE.

As noted earlier, PAR first arose in the international- and community-development context but was adapted in North America in response to the limitations of other approaches in social science research. A distinguishing feature of PAR in North America is that it seeks to help organizations change rather than just accumulating facts and examining implications (Whyte, 1991). Grounded in three streams of intellectual reasoning—social-research methodology, participation in decision making, and sociotechnical systems thinking— this version of PAR is distinct from those forms of participatory research that entail collaborative social science research with no action imperative (Tripp, 1990). A variant is participatory action science (Argyris and Schön, 1991), which focuses on theories-in-use, including strategies for uncovering organizational defensive routines. In the general PAR approach, stakeholders who are members of the target organization participate both as subjects of research and as co-researchers. PAR "aims at creating an environment in which participants give and get valid information, make free and informed choices (including the choice to participate) and generate internal commitment to the results of their inquiry" (Argyris and Schön, 1991, p. 86). Inasmuch as the goal of PAR is to inform and improve practice within organizations, the approach links well with P-PE. There is generally a partnership arrangement between researchers and organization members, and the organization members take an active role in a wide range of research activities.

Emancipatory action research (also called participatory action research by McTaggart, 1991a) is more closely associated with T-PE but differs in important ways. This approach stems from the work of Habermas and is expressly liberative because practitioners come together with critical intent (Carr and Kemmis, 1992). Power resides in the whole group, not with the facilitator or with individuals or stakeholders. The practitioner group accepts responsibility for its own emancipation from irrationality, injustice, alienation, and failure. A variant stream is called critical action research (Tripp, 1990), which is fully in sync with the sentiment but stops short of action. McTaggart (1991a) does not find the distinction useful. Although many of these attributes are shared with T-PE, this form of action research precludes the involvement of conventional researchers, who are viewed, at least potentially, as members of the power elite.

Finally cooperative inquiry (Heron, 1981; Reason and Heron, 1986), with its roots in humanistic psychology, is a form of research that arose in response to perceived deficiencies in orthodox approaches. In cooperative inquiry, "all those involved in the research are both co-researchers, whose thinking and decision making contribute to generating ideas, designing and managing the project, and drawing conclusions from the experience and *also* co-subjects, participating in the activity being researched" (emphasis in original, Reason, 1994, p. 326). Propositional knowledge about persons is derived both from their experiential knowledge and from practical knowledge concerns. Typically, the inquiry group is formed in response to the initiatives of certain parties or members, and therefore the group must struggle with internal issues of power, decision making, and practicality. To the extent that these issues are resolved internally, the group's work will be productive. In cooperative inquiry, trained researchers normally are not participants in the inquiry group. Participants engage in all phases of the inquiry process, including focusing, observing, reflecting, and deciding.

Issues and Questions

We end by posing a set of questions for consideration. These are not necessarily new, nor are they unique to PE as an approach to collaborative inquiry. Many of these issues are addressed in depth elsewhere in this volume.

Power and Its Ramifications. Who really controls the evaluation? How does one account for and deal with variation in power and influence among participants and between participants and the evaluator? How does one listen for the voices that have not yet been heard? How much should (or can) an outside evaluator meddle in the affairs of others, especially when these people need to live with the consequences long after the evaluator has left the scene?

Ethics. Closely related to issues of power and authority are issues of ethical conduct and ownership of data. Who owns the evaluation findings? Who has the power to dictate what data will be used and to what end? In what ways can participants with less power influence these decisions? In some instances, professional evaluators may witness the deliberate manipulation of data or other mischievous behavior by participants. At what point do evaluators draw the line and terminate their participation? Can or should evaluators just walk away from such situations?

Participant Selection. Who participates on the inquiry team, and how are participants identified and selected? The answers to these questions depend on the nature of power relationships within the context. What are the implications for participant selection when PE projects arise out of external mandates from funding agencies or organizations responsible for initiating such activities (or both)? What are the implications for participant selection in such cases? How many participants? How will they participate and at what juncture? A related concern is practical. In projects involving participants from a wide range of interest groups, to what extent is the feasibility of the project compromised?

Technical Quality. How is technical quality defined? By whom? Are there tensions related to data quality and the relevance of the evaluation to the local setting? What criteria ought to be used in deciding what to do in such a case? These questions are also related to issues of ownership and control.

Cross-Cultural Issues. How can cultural, language, or racial barriers be addressed? To what extent does the technical knowledge and background of the professional evaluator fit with the culture in question? Can the technical knowledge be adapted or made to fit, and if so, how?

Training. How is the training of participants in evaluation and research methods to be accomplished? Will training occur prior to the evaluation, during it, or by some combination of the two? To what extent do cultural and linguistic differences intrude on training effectiveness? Can evaluators and other professionals assume the role of trainer or facilitator with relative ease? What sorts of training should evaluators receive as they develop professionally and take on participatory projects? What knowledge and skills will be needed? Can the knowledge and skills be taught and, indeed, learned in formal in-service and preservice training environments?

Conditions Enabling PE. Finally we ask, what conditions need to be in place for meaningful PE to flourish? What should participants' backgrounds and interests be? What constraints will they bring to the task (workload considerations, educational limitations, motivation)? Who initiates the evaluation and why? What are the time constraints? How will these issues be addressed?

These are the challenges we see for participatory evaluators and people interested in engaging in such activities. Credible answers to these questions will come only from sustained PE practice and particularly from practice that includes deliberate mechanisms for ongoing observation and reflection. It is our hope that both participatory evaluators and the participants with whom they work will report on their experiences, thus informing professional understanding of these important issues.

References

African Development Foundation. *Participatory Evaluation Handbook: A Resource for Resident Evaluators.* Washington, D.C.: African Development Foundation, n.d.

Alkin, M. C. "Evaluation Theory Development: II." In M. W. McLaughlin and D. C. Phillips (eds.), *Evaluation and Education: At Quarter Century.* Chicago: University of Chicago Press, 1991.

Alvik, T. "School-Based Evaluation: A Close-Up." *Studies in Educational Evaluation,* 1995, *21,* 311–343.

Argyris, C., and Schön, D. A. "Participatory Action Research and Action Science: A Commentary." In W. F. Whyte (ed.), *Participatory Action Research.* Thousand Oaks, Calif.: Sage, 1991.

Ayers, T. D. "Stakeholders as Partners in Evaluation: A Stakeholder-Collaborative Approach." *Evaluation and Program Planning,* 1987, *10,* 263–271.

Brunner, I., and Guzman, A. "Participatory Evaluation: A Tool to Assess Projects and Empower People." In R. F. Conner and M. Hendricks (eds.), *International Innovations in Evaluation Methodology*. New Directions for Evaluation, no. 42. San Francisco: Jossey-Bass, 1989.

Bryk, A. S. (ed.) "Stakeholder-Based Evaluation." New Directions for Program Evaluation, no. 17. San Francisco: Jossey-Bass, 1983.

Campos, J. D. "Towards Participatory Evaluation: An Inquiry into Post-Training Experiences of Guatemalan Community Development Workers." Unpublished doctoral dissertation, University of Massachusetts, 1990.

Carr, W., and Kemmis, S. *Becoming Critical: Education, Knowledge and Action Research.* London: Falmer, 1992.

Chambers, R. *Whose Reality Counts? Putting the Last First.* London: Intermediate Technology Publications, 1997.

Comstock, D. E., and Fox, R. "Participatory Research as Critical Theory: The North Bonneville, USA Experience." In P. Park, M. Brydon-Miller, B. Hall, and T. Jackson (eds.), *Voices of Change: Participatory Research in the United States and Canada.* Toronto: OISE Press, 1993.

Coupal, F. "Participatory Project Design: Its Implications for Evaluation. A Case Study from El Salvador." Paper presented at the joint meeting of the Canadian Evaluation Society and the American Evaluation Association, Vancouver, Nov. 1995.

Cousins, J. B. "Assessing Program Needs Using Participatory Evaluation: A Comparison of High and Marginal Success Cases." In J. B. Cousins and L. M. Earl (eds.), *Participatory Evaluation in Education: Studies in Evaluation Use and Organizational Learning.* London: Falmer, 1995.

Cousins, J. B. "Consequences of Researcher Involvement in Participatory Evaluation." *Studies in Educational Evaluation*, 1996, 22(1), 3–27.

Cousins, J. B., Donohue, J. J., and Bloom, G. A. "Collaborative Evaluation in North America: Evaluators' Self-Reported Opinions, Practices and Consequences." *Evaluation Practice*, 1996, 17(3), 207–226.

Cousins, J. B., and Earl, L. M. "The Case for Participatory Evaluation." *Educational Evaluation and Policy Analysis*, 1992, 14(4), 397–418.

Cousins, J. B., and Earl, L. M. (eds.). *Participatory Evaluation in Education: Studies in Evaluation Use and Organizational Learning.* London: Falmer, 1995.

Ellis, D., Reid, G., and Barnsley, J. *Keeping on Track: An Evaluation Guide for Community Groups.* Vancouver: Women's Research Centre, 1990.

Fals-Borda, O. "Science and the Common People." Paper presented at the International Forum on Participatory Research, Ljubljana, Yugoslavia, 1980.

Fals-Borda, O., and Anisur-Rahman, M. *Action and Knowledge: Breaking the Monopoly with Participatory Action Research.* New York: Apex Press, 1991.

Fernandes, W., and Tandon, R. *Participatory Research and Evaluation: Experiments in Research as a Process of Liberation.* New Delhi: Indian Social Institute, 1981.

Fetterman, D. M. "Empowerment Evaluation." *Evaluation Practice*, 1994, 15(1), 1–15.

Fetterman, D. M. "In Response." *Evaluation Practice*, 1995, 16(2), 179–199.

Fetterman, D. M., Kaftarian, S. J., and Wandersman, A. *Empowerment Evaluation: Knowledge and Tools for Self Assessment and Accountability.* Thousand Oaks, Calif.: Sage, 1996.

Feuerstein, M.-T. *Partners in Evaluation: Evaluating Development and Community Programmes with Participants.* London: Macmillan, 1986.

Feuerstein, M.-T. "Finding the Methods to Fit the People: Training for Participatory Evaluation." *Community Development Journal*, 1988, 23, 16–25.

Forss, K. *Participatory Evaluation: Questions and Issues.* A report commissioned by the Central Evaluation Office, Occasional Paper 1. New York: United Nations Development Program, 1989.

Freedman, J. *Participatory Evaluations: Making Projects Work.* Technical Paper TP94/2. Calgary, Alberta: Division of International Development, International Centre, University of Calgary, 1994.

Freire, P. *Pedagogy of the Oppressed.* New York: Seabury Press, 1970.

Freire, P. "Creating Alternative Research Methods: Learning to Do It by Doing It." In B. Hall, A. Gillette, and R. Tandon (eds.), *Creating Knowledge: A Monopoly. Participatory Research in Development.* New Delhi: Society for Participatory Research in Asia, 1982.

Garaway, G. B. "Participatory Evaluation." *Studies in Educational Evaluation,* 1995, *21*(1), 85–102.

Gaventa, J. *Power and Powerlessness: Quiescence and Rebellion in an Appalachian Valley.* Chicago: University of Chicago Press, 1980.

Gaventa, J. "Land Ownership in Appalachia, USA: A Citizen's Research Project." In F. Dubell, T. Erasmie, and J. deVries (eds.), *Research for the People—Research by the People: Selected Papers from the International Forum on Participatory Research in Ljubljana, Yugoslavia.* Linkoping, Sweden: Linkoping University, 1981.

Gaventa, J. "Participatory Research in North America." *Convergence,* 1988, *24*(2–3), 19–28.

Gaventa, J. "The Powerful, the Powerless and the Experts: Knowledge Struggles in an Information Age." In P. Park, M. Brydon-Miller, B. Hall, and T. Jackson (eds.), *Voices of Change: Participatory Research in the United States and Canada.* Toronto: OISE Press, 1993.

Green, L. W., George, M. A., Daniel, M., Frankish, C. J., Herbert, C. J., Bowie, W. R., and O'Neill, M. *Study of Participatory Research in Health Promotion.* Vancouver: Royal Society of Canada, 1995.

Greene, J. G. "Stakeholder Participation and Utilization in Program Evaluation." *Evaluation Review,* 1988, *12*(2), 91–116.

Guba, E. G., and Lincoln, Y. S. *Fourth Generation Evaluation.* Thousand Oaks, Calif.: Sage, 1989.

Hall, B. L. *Creating Knowledge: Breaking the Monopoly.* Toronto: Participatory Research Group, International Council for Adult Education, 1977.

Hall, B. L. "Participatory Research, Popular Knowledge and Power: A Personal Reflection." *Convergence,* 1981, *14*(3), 6–19.

Hall, B. L. "From Margins to Center? The Development and Purpose of Participatory Research." *American Sociologist,* winter 1992, pp. 15–28.

Heron, J. "Validity in Co-operative Inquiry." In P. Reason (ed.), *Human Inquiry in Action.* London: Sage, 1981.

Huberman, M. "The Many Modes of Participatory Evaluation." In J. B. Cousins and L. M. Earl (eds.), *Participatory Evaluation in Education: Studies in Evaluation Use and Organizational Learning.* London: Falmer, 1995.

Huberman, M., and Cox, P. "Evaluation Utilization: Building Links Between Action and Reflection." *Studies in Educational Evaluation,* 1990, *16,* 157–179.

Jackson, E. T., and Kassam, Y. (eds.). *Better Knowledge, Better Results: Participatory Evaluation in Development Cooperation.* West Hartford: Kumarian Press, in press.

Jenlink, P. M. "Dialogue, Collective Inquiry and Organizational Learning: The Use of Focus-Group Methods for Learning." Paper presented at the annual meeting of the American Evaluation Association, Boston, Nov. 1994.

Kassam, Y., and Mustafa, K. *Participatory Research: An Emerging Alternative Methodology in Social Science Research.* Toronto: International Council for Adult Education, 1982.

King, J. A. "Research on Evaluation and Its Implications for Evaluation Research and Practice." *Studies in Educational Evaluation,* 1988, *14,* 285–299.

King, J. A. "Involving Practitioners in Evaluation Studies: How Viable Is Collaborative Evaluation in Schools?" In J. B. Cousins and L. M. Earl (eds.), *Participatory Evaluation in Education: Studies in Evaluation Use and Organizational Learning.* London: Falmer, 1995.

Lackey, A., Peterson, M., and Pine, J. "Participatory Evaluation: A Tool for Community Development Practitioners." *Journal of the Community Development Society*, 1981, 12(1), 83–102.

Lafleur, C. "A Participatory Approach to District-Level Program Evaluation: The Dynamics of Internal Evaluation." In J. B. Cousins and L. M. Earl (eds.), *Participatory Evaluation in Education: Studies in Evaluation Use and Organizational Learning*. London: Falmer, 1995.

Levin, B. "Collaborative Research in and with Organizations." *Qualitative Studies in Education*, 1993, 6(4), 331–340.

Leviton, L. C., and Hughes, E.F.X. "Research on the Utilization of Evaluations: A Review and Synthesis." *Evaluation Review*, 1981, 5(4), 525–548.

MacDonald, B. "Evaluation and the Control of Education." In D. A. Tawney (ed.), *Curriculum Evaluation Today: Trends and Implications*. Schools Council Research Studies. London: Macmillan, 1976.

Maguire, P. *Doing Participatory Research: A Feminist Approach*. Amherst, Mass.: Center for International Education, University of Massachusetts, 1987.

Mark, M. M., and Shotland, R. L. "Stakeholder-Based Evaluation and Value Judgments: The Role of Perceived Power and Legitimacy in the Selection of Stakeholder Groups." *Evaluation Review*, 1985, 9, 605–626.

Mathison, S. "Rethinking the Evaluator Role: Partnerships Between Organizations and Evaluators." *Evaluation and Program Planning*, 1994, 17(3), 299–304.

McTaggart, R. "Principles for Participatory Action Research." *Adult Education Quarterly*, 1991a, 41(3), 168–187.

McTaggart, R. "When Democratic Evaluation Doesn't Seem Democratic." *Evaluation Practice*, 1991b, 12(1), 9–21.

Nevo, D. "The Evaluation Minded School: An Application of Perceptions from Program Evaluation." *Evaluation Practice*, 1993, 14(1), 39–47.

Nevo, D. "Combining Internal and External Evaluation: A Case for School-Based Evaluation." *Studies in Educational Evaluation*, 1994, 20, 87–98.

Owen, J. M., and Lambert, F. C. "Roles for Evaluation in Learning Organizations." *Evaluation*, 1995, 1(2), 237–250.

Patton, M. Q. "Developmental Evaluation." *Evaluation Practice*, 1994, 15(3), 311–319.

Patton, M. Q. "Toward Distinguishing Empowerment Evaluation and Placing It in a Larger Context." *Evaluation Practice*, 1997a, 18(2), 147–163.

Patton, M. Q. *Utilization-Focused Evaluation*. (3rd ed.) Thousand Oaks, Calif.: Sage, 1997b.

Perry, P. D., and Backus, C. A. "A Different Perspective on Empowerment Evaluation: Benefits and Risks to the Evaluation Process." *Evaluation Practice*, 1995, 16(1), 37–46.

Preskill, H. "Evaluation's Role in Enhancing Organizational Learning." *Evaluation and Program Planning*, 1994, 17(3), 291–297.

Pursley, L. A. "Empowerment and Utilization Through Participatory Evaluation." Unpublished doctoral dissertation, Department of Human Service Studies, Cornell University, 1996.

Rappaport, J. "Terms of Empowerment/Exemplars of Prevention: Toward a Theory of Community Psychology." *American Journal of Community Psychology*, 1987, 15, 121–148.

Reason, P. "Three Approaches to Participative Inquiry," In N. K. Denzin and Y. S. Lincoln (eds.), *Handbook of Qualitative Research*. Thousand Oaks, Calif.: Sage, 1994.

Reason, P., and Heron, J. "Research with People: The Paradigm of Co-operative Experiential Inquiry." *Person Centered Review*, 1986, 1, 456–475.

Rugh, J. "Can Participatory Evaluation Meet the Needs of All Stakeholders? A Case Study Evaluating the World Neighbours West Africa Program." Paper presented at the annual meeting of the American Evaluation Association, Boston, Nov. 1994.

Shulha, L., and Cousins, J. B. "Utilization and Social Justice: Interconnections of Meta-Evaluation Frameworks." Paper presented at the joint meeting of the Canadian Evaluation Society and the American Evaluation Association, Vancouver, Nov. 1995.

Shulha, L. M., and Cousins, J. B. "Recent Developments in Theory and Research on Evaluation Utilization." Paper presented at the annual meeting of the American Evaluation Association, Atlanta, Ga., Nov. 1996.

Tandon, R. "Participatory Research in the Empowerment of People." *Convergence*, 1981, *14*(3), 20–29.

Tandon, R., and Fernandes, W. *Participatory Evaluation: Theory and Practice*. New Delhi: Indian Institute for Social Research, 1984.

Torres, R. T., Preskill, H. S., and Piontek, M. E. *Evaluation Strategies for Communicating and Reporting: Enhancing Learning in Organizations*. Thousand Oaks, Sage, 1996.

Tripp, D. H. "Socially Critical Action Research." *Theory into Practice*, 1990, *29*(3), 158–166.

United Nations Development Program. *Who Are the Question Makers? A Participatory Evaluation Handbook*. New York: Office of Evaluation and Strategic Planning, United Nations Development Program, 1997.

Weiss, C. H. "Utilization; of Evaluation: Toward Comparative Study." In C. H. Weiss (ed.), *Evaluating Action Programs: Readings in Social Action and Education*. Needham Heights, Mass.: Allyn & Bacon, 1972.

Weiss, C. H. "The Many Meanings of Research Utilization." *Public Administration Review*, 1979, *39*, 426–431.

Whitmore, E. "Participatory Approaches to Evaluation: Side Effects and Empowerment." Unpublished doctoral dissertation, Department of Human Service Studies, Cornell University, 1988.

Whitmore, E. "Evaluation and Empowerment: It's the Process That Counts." *Empowerment and Family Support Networking Bulletin* (Cornell University Empowerment Project), 1991, *2*(2), 1–7.

Whitmore, E. "To Tell the Truth: Working with Oppressed Groups in Participatory Approaches to Inquiry." In P. Reason (ed.), *Participation in Human Inquiry*. London: Sage, 1994.

Whyte, W. F. (ed.). *Participatory Action Research*. Thousand Oaks, Calif.: Sage, 1991.

At the time of publication J. BRADLEY COUSINS *was a professor of educational administration on the Faculty of Education and director of professional development programs at the University of Ottawa, Canada. He has written widely on education issues, evaluation use, and participatory evaluation. He coedited, with* Lorna Earl, Participatory Evaluation in Education: Studies in Evaluation Use and Organizational Learning.

At the time of publication ELIZABETH WHITMORE *was an associate professor at the School of Social Work at Carleton University in Ottawa, Canada. She discovered participatory research and evaluation while a graduate student at Cornell University and has since conducted a number of participatory evaluations. She has written numerous articles on this topic.*

This chapter examines coverage of cultural and underrepresented group issues in New Directions for Evaluation *over the last twenty years.*

New Directions for Evaluation Coverage of Cultural Issues and Issues of Significance to Underrepresented Groups

Anna Madison

This chapter examines coverage of cultural and underrepresented group issues in *New Directions for Evaluation* over the last twenty years. I have chosen not to use the term *minority* because of the historical political and social implications attached to the term. *Minority group* in American vernacular too often means *less than*. Instead of minority, the term *underrepresented group* is used to identify low-income, nonwhite ethnic and racial groups who have little or no input in policy, program, and evaluation decision making. The commonality among these groups is they are poor and share a history of political powerlessness, social oppression, and economic exploitation. Because of their socioeconomic status, they depend on governmental interventions and interventions sponsored by nonprofit philanthropic organizations to correct deficiencies in the allocation of societal resources.

Over the past twenty years several topics covered in NDE are relevant to underrepresented groups, including cultural sensitivity; cultural competence; stakeholder-based, responsive, democratic deliberation; and participatory evaluation theories, methodologies, and practices. Also, the topic of social justice and evaluation directly addresses evaluators' responsibility to ensure fairness to underrepresented groups. The analysis presented in this

NEW DIRECTIONS FOR EVALUATION, no. 114, Summer 2007 © Wiley Periodicals, Inc.
Published online in Wiley InterScience (www.interscience.wiley.com) • DOI: 10.1002/ev.227

chapter includes NDE issues and chapters that focus primarily on under-represented low-income, nonwhite ethnic and racial group issues in evaluation. The coverage in NDE is discussed by topical themes. If there are oversights, I apologize in advance.

Evaluation and Social Justice (Sirotnik, 1990), perhaps one of the most controversial NDE issues, is the first to make an important contribution to underrepresented groups in that the evaluation focus moves from individual and community to more fundamental issues of societal distributions of benefits and burdens. This issue advances the notion that social justice considerations in evaluation should serve the interests of marginalized, disenfranchised, and underrepresented groups. In this issue, Ericson argues that evaluators are in a unique position to set moral standards by which education and social programs are judged. He presents the proposition that social justice is the central moral standard that practitioners of evaluation should readily apply to social programs, practices, and institutions (1990, p. 6).

The social justice NDE issue represented a major departure from conventional thinking in the evaluation field. From the perspective of underrepresented groups, the value of the issue is that it placed evaluation at a crossroads by posing the questions: Will the profession accept its moral responsibilities to the underrepresented groups for whom redistributive social policy is designed to benefit in the first place? This issue has stimulated important debates in the profession about the role and function of evaluation that continue to this day. The democratic deliberation approach to evaluation, later introduced by House and Howe in NDE, addresses the equity issues raised in the issue on social justice.

Evaluation as a Democratic Process (Ryan and DeStefano, 2000) addresses democratic deliberative evaluation theory and practice. The democratic deliberation framework allows one to think of evaluation in relation to power differentials in the evaluation process that reflect the larger sociopolitical and moral structure. House and Howe argue, "Evaluation always existed within some authority structure, some particular social system. It does not stand alone as simply a logic or methodology, free of time and space, and is certainly not free of values or interests. Rather, evaluation practices are firmly embedded in and inextricably tied to particular social and institutional structures and practices" (2000, p. 3). House and Howe present a strong case for evaluation practices to include the voices of the less powerful, particularly low-income, nonwhite ethnic and racial groups. House and Howe suggest evaluators should represent their voices when they are not able to advocate for themselves.

This NDE issue is significant to underrepresented groups because the democratic deliberation approach offers a framework for the inclusion of their voices in the deliberation process. This approach is clearly aligned with the evaluator's responsibility for general and public welfare. However, Hood (2000) cautions it will be difficult to implement democratic deliberations in the African American population because subgroups of Americans have experienced democracy differently. He challenges the notion that deliberative processes can occur in underrepresented groups in the absence of evaluators who are representative of the group. Hood alleges that shared historical experience and common understandings and meanings about democracy and its utility could make a difference in one's willingness to engage in dialogue and deliberation.

Greene's (2000) and Torres's (2000) reflections on their attempts to include underrepresented groups in democratic dialogue and deliberations seem to support Hood's assertions. These evaluators suggest the democratic deliberation ideal is wonderful, but its implementation presents many challenges. Greene reports that inviting underrepresented groups to participate in the deliberation process does not necessarily mean that they will participate. Torres and her colleagues concluded the necessary conditions to include underrepresented groups in deliberations were not present in the evaluation environment. Due to time and money constraints, the program beneficiaries' voices were included only in data gathering. The central lesson from these reflections is that there are obstacles to implementing this approach. However, these evaluators stop short of saying that the inclusion of underrepresented groups in democratic deliberations is impossible.

Minority Issues in Program Evaluation (Madison, 1992) is the first NDE issue devoted to the relevance of culture in evaluation practice in urban, culturally diverse communities. The central theme of this issue is that program staff and evaluators cannot effectively evaluate social programs if they do not understand their sociopolitical and sociocultural context. Madison questions whether social problem solving and community change theory made sense in the absence of the voices of culturally diverse minorities. She asserts that culturally diverse underrepresented groups are in the best position to understand the effects of redistributive social policy on their lives. The chapters in this issue provide reflections on evaluators' experiences working in culturally diverse settings. The main argument is that inclusion of underrepresented groups in evaluations of education reform and social policy improves the evaluation and benefits the community. Baizerman and Compton (1992) also discuss the difficulty in knowing how well a program is working without including the voices of the people whose lives are most affected by public policy. They suggest that inclusion of low-income parents' and students' voices in evaluations can be liberating and empowering.

Other topics included in this issue are an examination of measurements that ignore culture, and the use of race as an explanatory variable. These topics are very much alive in current conversations of validity and scientific rigor in evaluation. The thread that bonds the chapters in this NDE issue is attention to the lack of cultural and contextual responsiveness in evaluation practice in low-income and nonwhite ethnic communities in the United States.

NEW DIRECTIONS FOR EVALUATION • DOI: 10.1002/ev

Hopson, Lucas, and Peterson (2000) advance the discussion of cultural sensitivity further by suggesting that cultural understanding should be a required competency to conduct evaluations in multicultural settings in the United States. In *How and Why Language Matters in Evaluation*, Hopson (2000) uses language to illustrate the importance of cultural understandings in evaluation in diverse cultural settings. An analysis of language used by program participants and the meaning assigned to their knowledge of HIV/AIDS is presented to demonstrate the importance of sensitivity to language in conducting evaluations of prevention programs. Also in this NDE issue, building on the theme presented in the 1992 NDE issue, Madison (2000) explores the sociocultural and sociopolitical nature of language and its use in program planning and evaluation of programs serving low-income, nonwhite ethnic groups. This NDE issue adds to the understanding that evaluation is culture-bound and language is one element of cultural understanding of the realities of racial and nonwhite ethnic groups.

The next NDE issue contributing to the discourse about cultural competence in evaluation is the one edited by Thompson-Robinson, Hopson, and SenGupta (2004). Integration of cultural competence into mainstream evaluation principles and practice is the central focus of *Cultural Competence in Evaluation*. The editors provide a comprehensive view of cultural competence, beginning with clarification of the concept in the context of evaluation, drawing from other disciplines. One of the most important features of this issue is that cultural competence is defined as a "skill set" fundamental to evaluation practice. The editors provide a compelling argument that the field of evaluation should incorporate cultural competence into the principles of evaluation practice.

In addition to providing a conceptual framework to understand cultural competency in the context of evaluation practice, case studies in this issue provide insight into cultural competence in practice in various ethnic groups. Each author presents the challenges to conducting culturally responsive evaluations and provides recommendations to improve cultural responsiveness.

Continuation of the cultural competency theme is presented in the *Critical Issues in STEM Evaluation* issue. Mertens and Hopson (2006) report that paying attention to diversity makes a difference in the overall quality of National Science Foundation STEM program evaluations. Also, they note that attention to diversity makes a difference in evaluation usefulness to improve programs designed to increase the representation of underrepresented groups in STEM professions.

Responsive evaluation theory and practice provide another opportunity to address issues relevant to underrepresented groups in NDE. Two chapters in the *Responsive Evaluation* NDE issue (Greene and Abma, 2001) focus on underrepresented groups. Wadsworth (2001) provides an example of successful responsive evaluation practice that included underrepresented groups. She departs from an end-user information-gathering approach to responsive evaluation. She interprets responsiveness to be "how" evaluators should work with local communities. She views responsiveness as a process through which all stakeholders are engaged in meaningful interaction and dialogue with evaluators. She asserts that this process results in the cocreation of evaluations for the purpose of learning and change. Hood's (2001) chapter in this issue discusses culture and race as important considerations in responsive evaluation. To ensure evaluations are responsive to racial and non-white ethnic groups, Hood suggests the evaluation profession should include more evaluators of color.

Mohan, Bernstein, and Whitsett (2002) are the editors of the NDE issue that discusses the political and institutional environments in which evaluations take place, including the local providers and end users of evaluation. Even though underrepresented group issues are not the issue focus, the issue provides insight into how groups can sabotage an evaluation, even though they have relatively little power in the political hierarchy in which education policy and program decisions are made. They note: "Parents are a key stakeholder group and have what might be called indirect authority; they can choose to block participation of their children in the evaluation—students can influence the accuracy and reliability of evaluation results, because they ultimately control the extent to which the information they provide is truthful and candid" (Guzman and Feria, 2002, p. 63). This chapter provides food for thought about the consequences of not including key local stakeholders in programming and evaluation decisions. This is important because there is very little discussion in the evaluation literature about the effects the disenfranchised can have on the overall quality of evaluations. The underlying message is that validity is likely to be compromised in education and social policy evaluations in which underrepresented groups are not included in the evaluation decision making process.

One of the strongest affirmations of the potential of the responsive approach to evaluation in urban communities is provided by Thomas and Stevens (2004), editors of *Co-Constructing a Contextually Responsive Evaluation Framework*. In this issue, they address the relevance of cultural competence as a fundamental skill in evaluation, focusing on contextual responsiveness. The editors encourage evaluators to be self-reflective and to be open to examining their own assumptions and stereotypes about urban schools and their stakeholders because individuals' attitudes make a difference in contextually responsive evaluations. The chapters in this issue report on evaluations of urban school reform programs situated in a low-income urban community, affirming that a deep respect for the importance of culture and situational responsiveness are crucial steps to conduct useful, valid evaluations that foster learning and inspire community change.

Thomas's chapter in this issue stands apart from other examples of responsive evaluation in underrepresented groups. She provides a real-world case example of successful contextually and culturally responsive evaluations in urban low-income, nonwhite ethnic communities that include the voices of parents and students. Thomas demonstrates that the co-construction approach to evaluation can lead to meaningful school reform. The co-construction process is very much about valuing. She states, "Co-construction, by necessity, involves a redistribution of power, assuming a kind of equality among different stakeholders. It seeks to democratize the evaluation process by lessening the implicit, and sometime explicit power dynamics between evaluators and project stakeholders" (Thomas, 2004, p. 9). This review of NDE coverage of issues relevant to underrepresented groups reveals that there has been an increase in NDE content on topics of interest to underrepresented groups. With increases in the representation of nonwhite ethnic and cultural diversity in the evaluation profession, it is likely that this trend will continue.

Over the last twenty years there have been three issues devoted to the multicultural and multiethnic dimension of evaluation practice in the United States. The recent focus on cultural competence in NDE can largely be attributed to the increased diversity of the AEA membership and the work of the AEA Diversity Committee.

The unifying theme of NDE issues that address cultural sensitivity, cultural responsiveness, and cultural competence is that cultural competence and cultural responsiveness do make a difference in evaluation outcomes and evaluation's utilization. There is consensus that if evaluations are to foster learning for improvements in local communities, they must be contextually and culturally responsive. The authors acknowledge that one of the main challenges in conducting evaluations across cultures is the investment in time; however, there is agreement among them that the investment in time is worth the long-term yield.

Stakeholder-based, responsive, democratic deliberation tenets, theories, and methodologies can be placed under the rubric of participatory evaluation. The appearance of these concepts in the evaluation literature marked a turning point in the evaluation field. Participatory evaluation is based on the assumption that inclusion of multiple voices in planning and evaluation enhances learning. The philosophical, theoretical, and methodological foundation for this new direction in evaluation redefined the purpose of evaluation and its role in a democratic society. Until this departure, evaluation was very much a "technocratic endeavor." Evaluators were detached from the realities of the communities in which the programs they evaluated were implemented.

The shortcoming in the NDE coverage of participatory approaches to evaluation is that stakeholder, for the most part, does not include underrepresented poor, racial, and nonwhite ethnic groups. With the exception of NDE issues 45, 53, 85, 101, and 102, and the select chapters included in this review, *stakeholder* refers to program staff and community influential persons, who act as proxies for program beneficiaries. A common theme in NDE issues that has addressed participatory approaches to evaluation is that inclusion of underrepresented groups is desirable but difficult to achieve.

These NDE authors point out the cost constraints (money and time) and environmental conditions that are obstacles to including program beneficiaries as stakeholders.

Coverage of participatory and responsive evaluation in NDE reveals a large split between evaluators who share the "lived experiences" of underrepresented nonwhite racial and ethnic groups and most mainstream evaluators. Whereas most mainstream evaluators view inclusion as desirable, evaluators of color maintain that the inclusion of program beneficiaries in all aspects of the evaluation is the only way to conduct critical inquiry for social change. Inclusion of underrepresented groups is not only desirable, but imperative.

NDE coverage of cultural and underrepresented group issues illuminates the discrepancy between the ideals of evaluators that promote inclusion of the disenfranchised and the recognition of evaluation's responsibility to social justice, and the realities of evaluation practice. Overall, underrepresented groups continue to be presented as *subjects of evaluation* rather than as *invested stakeholders*.

References

Baizerman, M., and Compton, D. "From Respondent and Informant to Consultant and Participant: The Evolution of a State Agency Policy Evaluation." In A. Madison (ed.), *Minority Issues in Program Evaluation*. New Directions for Program Evaluation, no. 53. San Francisco: Jossey-Bass, 1992.

Ericson, D. P. "Social Justice, Evaluation, and the Educational System." *Evaluation and Social Justice: Issues in Public Education*. New Directions for Evaluation, no. 45. San Francisco: Jossey-Bass, 1990.

Greene, J. C. "Challenges in Practicing Deliberative Democratic Evaluation." In K. E. Ryan and L. DeStefano (eds.), *Evaluation as a Democratic Process: Promoting Inclusion, Dialogue, and Deliberation*. New Directions for Evaluation, no. 85. San Francisco: Jossey-Bass, 2000.

Greene, J. C., and Abma, T. A. (eds.). *Responsive Evaluation*. New Directions for Evaluation, no. 92. San Francisco: Jossey-Bass, 2001.

Guzman, B. L., and Feria, A. "Community-Based Organizations and State Initiatives: The Negotiation Process of Program Evaluation." In R. Mohan, D. J. Bernstein, and M. Whitsett (eds.), *Responding to Sponsors and Stakeholders in Complex Evaluation Environments*. New Directions for Evaluation, no. 95. San Francisco: Jossey-Bass, 2002.

Hood, S. "Commentary on Deliberative Democratic Evaluation." In K. E. Ryan and L. DeStefano (eds.), *Evaluation as a Democratic Process: Promoting Inclusion, Dialogue, and Deliberation*. New Directions for Evaluation, no. 85. San Francisco: Jossey-Bass, 2000.

Hood, S. "Nobody Knows My Name: In Praise of African American Evaluators Who Were Responsive." In J. C. Greene and T. A. Abma (eds.), *Responsive Evaluation*. New Directions for Evaluation, no. 92. San Francisco: Jossey-Bass, 2001.

Hopson, R. (ed.). *How and Why Language Matters in Evaluation*. New Directions for Evaluation, no. 86. San Francisco: Jossey-Bass, 2000.

Hopson, R., Lucas, K. J., and Peterson, J. "HIV/AIDS Talk: Implications for Prevention Intervention." In R. Hopson (ed.), *How and Why Language Matters in Evaluation*. New Directions for Evaluation, no. 86. San Francisco: Jossey-Bass, 2000.

House, E. R. and Howe, K. R. "Deliberative Democratic Evaluation." In K. E. Ryan and L. DeStefano (eds.), *Evaluation as a Democratic Process: Promoting Inclusion, Dialogue, and Deliberation.* New Directions for Evaluation, no. 85. San Francisco: Jossey-Bass, 2000.

Huffman, D., and Lawrenz, F. (eds.). *Critical Issues in STEM Evaluation.* New Directions for Evaluation, no. 109. San Francisco: Jossey-Bass, 2006.

Madison, A. M. (ed.). *Minority Issues in Program Evaluation.* New Directions for Program Evaluation, no. 53. San Francisco: Jossey-Bass, 1992.

Madison, A. M. "Language in Defining Social Problems and in Evaluating Social Programs." In R. Hopson (ed.), *How and Why Language Matters in Evaluation.* New Directions for Evaluation, no. 86. San Francisco: Jossey-Bass, 2000.

Mertens, D. M., and Hopson, R. K. "Advancing Evaluation STEM Efforts Through Attention to Diversity and Culture." In D. Huffman and F. Lawrenz (eds.), *Critical Issues in STEM Evaluation.* New Directions for Evaluation, no. 109. San Francisco: Jossey-Bass, 2006.

Mohan, R., Bernstein, D. J., and Whitsett, M. (eds.). *Responding to Sponsors and Stakeholders in Complex Evaluation Environments.* New Directions for Evaluation, no. 95. San Francisco: Jossey-Bass, 2002.

Ryan, K. E., and DeStefano, L. (eds.). *Evaluation as a Democratic Process: Promoting Inclusion, Dialogue, and Deliberation.* New Directions for Evaluation, no. 85. San Francisco: Jossey-Bass, 2000.

Sirotnik, E. A. (ed.). *Evaluation and Social Justice: Issues in Public Education.* New Directions for Program Evaluation, no. 45. San Francisco: Jossey-Bass, 1990.

Thomas, V. G. "Building a Contextually Responsive Evaluation Framework: Lessons from Working with Urban School Interventions." In V. G. Thomas and F. I. Stevens (eds.), *Co-Constructing a Contextually Responsive Evaluation Framework.* New Directions for Evaluation, no. 101. San Francisco: Jossey-Bass, 2004.

Thomas, V. G., and Stevens, F. I. (eds.). *Co-Constructing a Contextually Responsive Evaluation Framework.* New Directions for Evaluation, no. 101. San Francisco: Jossey-Bass, 2004.

Thompson-Robinson, M., Hopson, R., and SenGupta, S. (eds.). *Cultural Competence in Evaluation: Toward Principles and Practices.* New Directions for Evaluation, no. 102. San Francisco: Jossey-Bass, 2004.

Torres, R. T., Padilla Stone, S., Butkus, D. L., Hook, B. B., Casey, J., and Arens, S. A. "Dialogue and Reflection in a Collaborative Evaluation: Stakeholder and Evaluator Voices." In K. E. Ryan and L. DeStefano (eds.), *Evaluation as a Democratic Process: Promoting Inclusion, Dialogue, and Deliberation.* New Directions for Evaluation, no. 85. San Francisco: Jossey-Bass, 2000.

Wadsworth, Y. "Becoming Responsive—Some Consequences for Evaluation as Dialogue Across Distance." In J. C. Greene and T. A. Abma (eds.), *Responsive Evaluation.* New Directions for Evaluation, no. 92. San Francisco: Jossey-Bass, 2001.

ANNA MADISON is a professor in the College of Public and Community Service at the University of Massachusetts, Boston. She has for many years advocated for underrepresented groups in AEA and society.

At the twentieth birthday of the American Evaluation
Association, its twentieth-year president looks back at the
growth of the association and the field of evaluation, and
identifies where AEA and evaluation might go in
the future.

AEA and Evaluation:
2006 (and Beyond)

Melvin M. Mark

When it comes to markers of time, round numbers have a way of stimulating reflection. A fortieth or a fiftieth birthday, for instance, often leads people
to think about their lives, where they have been, and where they are going.
Similarly, *New Directions for Evaluation* editor Sandra Mathison has taken
the American Evaluation Association's (AEA) twentieth anniversary as the
occasion for a series of reflections. Because I had the honor of serving as
the twentieth president of AEA, Sandra invited me into the reflective process.
A critic might question whether AEA's twentieth anniversary truly warrants
this reflection. After all, AEA resulted from the merger of two predecessor
organizations, the Evaluation Research Society and the Evaluation Network,
which had been holding a joint conference for several years prior to the
formal merger. Perhaps the anniversary of either prior organization would be
a better occasion for reflection. Or, the critic might suggest, serious reflection about evaluation would better be tied to another marker from the early
history of contemporary evaluation. Candidates would include mandates for
evaluation in Great Society legislation, such as the Manpower Development
and Training Act of 1962 or Title I of the Elementary and Secondary Education Act of 1965, or the 1967 publication of E. A. Suchman's early book on
evaluation research.

Such criticisms have at least a grain of truth. As a relatively young
member of the field, not involved in association governance at the time,
I found the formal birth of AEA only modestly noticeable. The formal

NEW DIRECTIONS FOR EVALUATION, no. 114, Summer 2007   © Wiley Periodicals, Inc.
Published online in Wiley InterScience (www.interscience.wiley.com) • DOI: 10.1002/ev.228

citations to conference presentations changed. Conference conversations occasionally veered to the state of the merger. But it seems fair to say that the formation of AEA was a point in a line, not a sharp turn in the development of evaluation.

Such criticism misses the point, however. Engaging in occasional reflection has value, whatever the stimulus to reflection may be. The critic would also miss the point in another way. Although the birth of AEA may not have been a revolutionary event in the history of evaluation, professional associations do—or at least can and should—matter. Thus, reflection about the status, history, and potential of AEA itself is appropriate.

Having engaged in "metareflection," I turn now to the task at hand. First I offer some relatively brief reflections about AEA and then about the field of evaluation in general. Drawing on those observations, I conclude by pondering some possible directions for the future.

The Status of AEA

By many key indicators AEA is in the best shape ever. For many years membership has been growing, averaging over 10 percent growth per annum in the new millennium and reaching a total over five thousand at the end of our twentieth-anniversary year. This growth has taken place without any real efforts to expand the membership. The operational side of AEA is excellent by all reports, especially since we hired Susan Kistler, now executive director. The association is in very good shape financially, holding reserves beyond the amount most often specified for association "self-insurance."

These positive indicators are especially noteworthy because historically AEA has seen some hard times. In contrast to the current financial solvency, for many years the association lived hand to mouth. I served on the board at the time of the 1995 international conference in Vancouver. Given the higher level of investment in that conference, if it had failed financially AEA's very existence would have been at risk. Soon after that, AEA had the bad luck of hiring a well-recommended professional association management company just as it imploded, which damaged such basic things as dues collection and the membership list. Earlier, the financial consequences of the 1989 conference in San Francisco, which occurred during the earthquake, had threatened the association. A more complete history of AEA would identify other ups and downs, as well as multiple heroes.

The shift in AEA's financial situation, especially coupled with sound professional management services, is not trivial. Member services can be enhanced, as with the recent addition of electronic access to two more journals without increasing member dues or fees. New initiatives are feasible. During a previous term on the board, I saw potentially meritorious proposals that could not be seriously considered simply because the association could not afford them. Today, AEA can try new things, take risks, and consider proposals on their merit. Financial security matters.

There also have been ongoing changes in association governance. Among these are efforts across several years for the board to think more strategically, to link its decisions to broader considerations of AEA's mission, vision, and values. We have been more explicitly talking about "trialing" initiatives. Another subtle, but I think quite important change began, I believe, with the presidency of Dick Krueger and strengthened by Nick Smith and Sharon Rallis. Since then, there has been an effort to consult across the past president, president, and president-elect. This approach allows for more cumulative and productive governance, especially given that most things of real value cannot be achieved in a single year in an organization like AEA. This coordination across presidents can also avoid the wasted effort and whiplash that I believe occasionally occurred in years past when a new president brought in an agenda inconsistent with that of the old president. Although this consultative and collaborative process may be tenuous, subject to death at the hands of a single headstrong individual, I believe it is serving the association well and will bear fruit for years to come.

Evaluation Today

Many thoughtful members of the evaluation community have commented on the state of evaluation today. To provide references to all of their writings would alone exceed the page limit for this brief commentary. With gratitude, then, to pensive scholars and trenchant observers, let me try to summarize a few of the key trends in evaluation today. I will not try to identify all the important trends, but focus on a select set related to potential directions for the future.

First, evaluation seems to be increasingly common, often integrated into other related functions and not always labeled as evaluation. Second, individuals from varied backgrounds conduct evaluation in its various forms. These people often are unfamiliar with what many of us would call the evaluation literature or with AEA as an organization. Third, the role of evaluation in the world, including the potential for evaluation use and influence, has become more complex. Some developments, such as the creation of "approved lists" of programs, may increase use, whether appropriate or not. Other developments may act against evaluation use, including the emergence of partisan think tanks, the decline in the perceived authority of "evidence," and the challenges of getting good and understandable information in the hands of multiple parties, including the public.

Looking Forward

Although reflecting on yesterday and today can have many consequences, the most important ones involve how we think about tomorrow. With that in mind, I offer only a few of many possible suggestions for AEA and evaluation in the future.

First, collectively we should discuss, debate, and disseminate what the "value-added" is of an AEA-style approach to evaluation. Why should an evaluation funder be interested in someone with a background in evaluation, rather than someone from many of the other fields that offer the same services? What would a practitioner from these other fields gain from learning more about evaluation, its theories, its literature, its associations, and community? There are good answers, I believe. But unless we have them ready to share, evaluation practice may increasingly be done by people unfamiliar with what many of us think of as core ideas about evaluation.

Second, we should consider how to deal with what has been called the "empty chair" problem—that is, the general absence in AEA (or other evaluation associations, such as the European Evaluation Society) of economists and of many others who are doing evaluation. Our response might involve targeted recruitment. Or it might involve interassociation partnerships, dissemination of the value-added by an AEA-style evaluation background, or some other response. Alternatively, further consideration might lead to the conclusion that the empty chair is not a problem with which we wish to deal. At the very least, it calls for thoughtful discussion. And how we answer could substantially affect what AEA looks like in the future.

Third, we should work to expand the public presence of AEA. "Public" here is multifaceted, including the following examples: (a) not all people doing evaluation need to be AEA members, but it would be good if most were aware of AEA and saw us as a valuable resource; (b) AEA could be a more visible source of information to evaluation consumers, funders, the public, and the press; and (c) one can imagine a future in which if, say, a federal agency is considering regulations that will affect evaluation practice, it would contact AEA for experts and input.

In addition to the three future directions just mentioned, several more are worth attention. These include (but certainly are not limited to) increasing the evidence base about evaluation itself; updating our ideas and practices about evaluation use (or influence), especially in light of the changing world of decision making as illustrated by the What Works Clearinghouse; pondering the nature of evaluation and the role of AEA amidst globalization and the international growth of evaluation; thinking about better evaluation systems in government and other organizations; facilitating the responsiveness of evaluators to the varying evaluation needs of different contexts; enhancing and recognizing the work of those who strive to fulfill different roles related to evaluation as an endeavor, including practitioners, teachers, theorists, methodologists, and those who do research on evaluation; and considering alternative models of the relationship between AEA and its local affiliates. Some of these are the purview of AEA as an association. For others, advances may come at the hands of AEA members, using the forum provided by AEA, its conferences, journals, and other vehicles, such as the new public forum session that was initiated on a trial basis at the twentieth-anniversary conference.

Conclusion

The NDE chapters that are reprinted in this issue vividly illustrate a kind of contribution that AEA has made in its twenty years of existence. AEA, through its publications and conference, has been a forum for advances, debates, discussion, and community. That is not trivial. Nor is it all that AEA has accomplished. But today AEA seems poised for more and larger impacts, whether increasing its public presence or reflecting on whether and how to engage audiences beyond its membership. It will be interesting to see what people say when asked to reflect back during the thirtieth, fortieth, and fiftieth anniversaries of AEA.

Reference

Suchman, E. A. *Evaluation Research: Principles and Practices in Public Service and Social Programs.* New York: Russell Sage Foundation, 1967.

MELVIN M. MARK *is professor of psychology at Penn State University and immediate past president of the American Evaluation Association.*

INDEX

NEW DIRECTIONS FOR EVALUATION
Order Form
SUBSCRIPTIONS AND SINGLE ISSUES

DISCOUNTED BACK ISSUES:

Use this form to receive **20% off** all back issues of New Directions for Evaluation. All single issues priced at **$21.60** (normally $27.00)

TITLE	ISSUE NO.	ISBN
_____	_____	_____
_____	_____	_____
_____	_____	_____

Call 888-378-2537 or see mailing instructions below. When calling, mention the promotional code, JB7ND, to receive your discount.

SUBSCRIPTIONS: *(1 year, 4 issues)*

☐ New Order   ☐ Renewal

U.S.	☐ Individual: $80	☐ Institutional: $199
Canada/Mexico	☐ Individual: $80	☐ Institutional: $239
All Others	☐ Individual: $104	☐ Institutional: $273

Call 888-378-2537 or see mailing and pricing instructions below. Online subscriptions are available at www.interscience.wiley.com.

Copy or detach page and send to:
**John Wiley & Sons, Journals Dept, 5th Floor
989 Market Street, San Francisco, CA 94103-1741**

Order Form can also be faxed to: 888-481-2665

Issue/Subscription Amount: $ _____	**SHIPPING CHARGES:**
Shipping Amount: $ _____	SURFACE Domestic Canadian
(for single issues only—subscription prices include shipping)	First Item $5.00 $6.00
Total Amount: $ _____	Each Add'l Item $3.00 $1.50

(No sales tax for U.S. subscriptions. Canadian residents, add GST for subscription orders. Individual rate subscriptions must be paid by personal check or credit card. Individual rate subscriptions may not be resold as library copies.)

☐ Payment enclosed (U.S. check or money order only. All payments must be in U.S. dollars.)

☐ VISA ☐ MC ☐ Amex # _____ Exp. Date _____

Card Holder Name _____ Card Issue # _____

Signature_____ Day Phone _____

☐ Bill Me (U.S. institutional orders only. Purchase order required.)

Purchase order # _____
Federal Tax ID13559302   GST 89102 8052

Name_____

Address _____

Phone _____ E-mail _____

JB7ND

Other Titles Available

NEW DIRECTIONS FOR CHILD AND ADOLESCENT DEVELOPMENT SERIES
Sandra Mathison, Editor-in-Chief

For a complete list of back issues, please visit www.josseybass.com/go/ev

EV 113   **Informing Federal Policies on Evaluation Methodology: Building the Evidence Base for Method Choice in Government Sponsored Evaluation**
George Julnes, Debra J. Rog, Editors
This volume seeks to provide a space for a more productive dialogue that, by identifying areas of agreement but also fundamental differences, will promote a more durable working consensus on the circumstances in which some methods are to be preferred over others. The chapter authors and discussants make clear that there are different types of evidence with which to inform this dialogue, including empirical findings of the impact of method choice on evaluation outcomes, the evidence contained in the wisdom of practice, and the results of critical analyses of the broader social impacts of method choice. The editors build on these contributions to suggest pragmatic policies for federal agencies, promoting both context-appropriate method choice and the importance of managing portfolios of evaluative research that maintain desired distributions of methodologies.
ISBN 978-07879-97342

EV 112   **Promoting the Use of Government Evaluations in Policymaking**
Rakesh Mohan, Kathleen Sullivan, Editors
This volume explores management of the politics of evaluation, which an be accomplished by considering the context in which an evaluation occurs and examining strategies for maximizing both evaluators' independence from and their responsiveness to key stakeholders. Unconventional approaches, such as prospective evaluation and development of analytical tools for use by agency personnel, are examined, as is promotion of evaluation use through a symbiotic relationship with performance measurement. The chapter authors discuss utilization strategies as applied to evaluations of public health, education, and corrections programs. The final chapter provides sage advice to evaluators on how to impact policy development.
ISBN 978-07879-97083

(STEM) programs, with special emphasis on evaluation of STEM education initiatives. STEM evaluation has always been important, given the issues facing public schools and the economic and social considerations of STEM fields. But because these fields today face a variety of concerns, this discussion of STEM evaluation is particularly timely. Evaluation advances may contribute to STEM fields by helping programs address the challenges they face. This volume presents multiple viewpoints and state-of-the-art examples and methodological approaches in the hope that its chapters will contribute to the understanding of STEM evaluation, STEM education, STEM education evaluation, and evaluation in general. Overall, this volume of *New Directions for Evaluation* may help not only to move the field to consider new methods and methodologies for engaging in evaluation but also to reconsider ideas of what it means to engage in scientific evaluation.
ISBN 978-07879-85882

EV 108   **Evaluating Nonformal Education Programs and Settings**
Emma Norland, Cindy Somers, Editors
This volume explores the issues with which evaluators of nonformal education programs (such as parks, zoos, community outreach organizations, and museums) struggle. These issues are not unique to nonformal programs and settings. Rather, they pose different sets of problems and solutions from those that face evaluators of traditional education programs. The authors address this topic from extensive experience as evaluators and education professionals who have worked in nonformal education settings.
ISBN 978-07879-85424

EV 107   **Social Network Analysis in Program Evaluation**
Maryann M. Durland, Kimberly A Fredericks, Editors
This important issue of *New Directions for Evaluation* highlights social network analysis (SNA) methodology and its application within program evaluation. The application of SNA is relatively new for mainstream evaluation, and like most other innovations, it has yet to be fully explored in this field. The volume aims to fill the gaps within SNA methodology exploration by first reviewing the foundations and development of network analysis within the social sciences and the field of evaluation. The focus then turns to the methodology. Who holds power in a network, and what measures indicate whether that power is direct or indirect? Which subgroups have formed, and where are they positioned in an organization? How divided is an organization? Who forms the core of a collaboration, and where are the experts in an organization? These are the types of common questions

(STEM) programs, with special emphasis on evaluation of STEM education initiatives. STEM evaluation has always been important, given the issues facing public schools and the economic and social considerations of STEM fields. But because these fields today face a variety of concerns, this discussion of STEM evaluation is particularly timely. Evaluation advances may contribute to STEM fields by helping programs address the challenges they face. This volume presents multiple viewpoints and state-of-the-art examples and methodological approaches in the hope that its chapters will contribute to the understanding of STEM evaluation, STEM education, STEM education evaluation, and evaluation in general. Overall, this volume of *New Directions for Evaluation* may help not only to move the field to consider new methods and methodologies for engaging in evaluation but also to reconsider ideas of what it means to engage in scientific evaluation.
ISBN 978-07879-85882

EV 108   **Evaluating Nonformal Education Programs and Settings**
Emma Norland, Cindy Somers, Editors
This volume explores the issues with which evaluators of nonformal education programs (such as parks, zoos, community outreach organizations, and museums) struggle. These issues are not unique to nonformal programs and settings. Rather, they pose different sets of problems and solutions from those that face evaluators of traditional education programs. The authors address this topic from extensive experience as evaluators and education professionals who have worked in nonformal education settings.
ISBN 978-07879-85424

EV 107   **Social Network Analysis in Program Evaluation**
Maryann M. Durland, Kimberly A Fredericks, Editors
This important issue of *New Directions for Evaluation* highlights social network analysis (SNA) methodology and its application within program evaluation. The application of SNA is relatively new for mainstream evaluation, and like most other innovations, it has yet to be fully explored in this field. The volume aims to fill the gaps within SNA methodology exploration by first reviewing the foundations and development of network analysis within the social sciences and the field of evaluation. The focus then turns to the methodology. Who holds power in a network, and what measures indicate whether that power is direct or indirect? Which subgroups have formed, and where are they positioned in an organization? How divided is an organization? Who forms the core of a collaboration, and where are the experts in an organization? These are the types of common questions

explored in the four case studies of the use of network analysis within an evaluative framework. These cases are diverse in their evaluation situations and in the application of measures, providing a basis to model common applications of network analysis within the field. The final chapters include a personal account of current use by a government agency and suggestions for the future use of SNA for evaluation practice.
ISBN 978-07879-83949

EV 106   **Theorists' Models in Action**
Marvin Alkin, Christina A. Christie, Editors
This volume analyzes how evaluation theorists apply their approach in practice. A scenario of a situation at an elementary school is presented to four prominent theorists, who describe how they would design and conduct an evaluation of the school's program. The editors consider the theorists' proposed evaluations, as well as their subsequent comments, to develop themes related to the influence of theory and context on practice. They also provide a comparative analysis of the theorists' evaluation approaches in relation to the context of evaluation case presented. This volume demonstrates why evaluators need to adapt their point of view to a particular situation, and provides much-needed study and analysis on the way in which they make those adaptations.
ISBN 978-07879-82126

EV 105   **Teaching Evaluation Using the Case Method**
Michael Quinn Patton, Patricia Patrizi, Editors
The absence of readily available teaching cases has been a significant gap in the field of evaluation. This volume aims to begin filling that gap by presenting high-quality evaluation cases developed specifically for use with the case method. The volume begins by reviewing evaluation issues that cases can be used to surface and provides guidance for using the case method. Three in-depth cases are then presented for quite different evaluation situations. Each has been taught, field-tested, and refined in line with participant feedback. Each case ends with teaching questions and key evaluation points those questions are aimed at elucidating. Following the case chapters, a professional evaluator reflects on his experiences with the cases and offers lessons learned about evaluation teaching and training, including exercises for extrapolating lessons, illuminating ethical dilemmas, understanding and applying alternative evaluation models, and conducting metaevaluations, among other uses.
ISBN 978-07879-80160

EV 104   **International Perspectives on Evaluation Standards**
Craig Russon, Gabrielle Russon, Editors
Prior to 1995, there were fewer than half a dozen regional and
national evaluation organizations around the world. Today there
are more than fifty, attesting to a growing interest in the practice
of program evaluation internationally. Many of these new
organizations have undertaken efforts to develop their own
standards or to modify existing sets—most typically, the Program
Evaluation Standards of the Joint Committee on Standards for
Educational Evaluation—for use in their own cultural context.
Following two introductory chapters, one a conceptual overview
and the second a history of the development and revisions of the
Program Evaluation Standards, this issue documents standards
development efforts in three different settings: Western Europe,
Africa, and Australasia. In addition, because nongovernmental
organizations and governments have entered the standard-setting
business, other chapters describe standards development
activities by the European Commission and CARE International.
The content points to the challenge of formalizing standards for
program evaluation given cross-cultural differences in values and
to the continuing challenges related to implementing voluntary
standards.
ISBN 978-07879-78587

EV 103   **Global Advances in HIV/AIDS Monitoring and Evaluation**
Deborah Rugg, Greet Peersman, Michael Carael
The focus of this issue is on global advances in conducting
monitoring and evaluation (M&E) of the global response to the
HIV/AIDS epidemic. Only by implementing comprehensive and
sustainable M&E systems will we know how much progress we
are making, as nations and as a global community, in combating
this pandemic. The chapters primarily focus on developing
nations and are presented largely from the perspective of
evaluators working for donors, international agencies, and
national governments. Although it is clear that a comprehensive
M7E system must eventually include both monitoring and
evaluation, the initial aim has been to establish a foundation
derived largely from surveys and monitoring information. To
date, much of the focus in M&E has come from the global level
because new global funding intiatives been launched and
required rapid scale-up and the development of technical
guidance, international standards, and indicators for monitoring
progress and determining success. At the regional and country
levels, the challenge has been to implement national M&E plans
and systems within a context of overall low M&E capacity and a
range of M&E needs.
ISBN 978-07879-77801

EV 102 **In Search of Cultural Competence in Evaluation: Toward Principles and Practice**
Melva Thompson-Robinson, Rodney Hopson, Saumitra SenGupta, Editors

This volume focuses on culturally competent evaluation. The chapters address a number of questions: How does culture matter in evaluation theory and practice? How does attention to cultural issues make for better evaluation practice? How does attention to cultural issues make for better evaluation practice? What is the "value-addedness" of cultural competence in evaluation? How do the complexities, challenges, and politics of diversity issue affect evaluation? The first chapter is an overview of culture, cultural competence, and culturally competent evaluation; the other chapters provide case studies on the implementation of culturally competent evaluation in a variety of settings and with several populations. The volume contributors also present lessons learned from their experiences and recommendations for implementing cultural competent evaluations in general. This volume is part of an important discussion of race, culture, and diversity in evaluation striving to shape and advance culturally competent evaluation, and, in tandem, evaluation of culturally competent services.
ISBN 978-07879-76545

EV 101 **Co-Constructing a Contextually Responsive Evaluation Framework: The Talent Development Model of Reform**
Veronica G. Thomas, Floraline I. Stevens, Editors

This volume presents the Talent Development evaluation framework, an approach for evaluating urban school reform interventions deeply embedded in the work of the Howard University Center for Research on the Education of Students Placed At Risk (CRESPAR) and the Talent Development Model of School Reform. The CRESPAR Talent Development (TD) evaluation approach is rooted in several traditions of evaluation that intentionally seek engagement with contexts of practice. These traditions include responsive, participatory, empowerment, and culturally competent approaches to evaluation. The CRESPAR TD evaluation approach also takes up themes of inclusiveness and partnership advanced by the recent promotion of multiple methods in evaluation. With these themes, the TD evaluation approach is viably grounded in well-accepted evaluation concepts and principles. The approach further seeks to be practical, useful, formative, and empowering for the many individuals served by TD evaluations and to give "voice" to persons whose perspectives are often ignored, minimized, or rejected in urban school settings.
ISBN 978-07879-74534

NEW DIRECTIONS FOR EVALUATION
IS NOW AVAILABLE ONLINE AT WILEY INTERSCIENCE

What is Wiley InterScience?

Wiley InterScience is the dynamic online content service from John Wiley & Sons delivering the full text of over 300 leading scientific, technical, medical, and professional journals, plus major reference works, the acclaimed Current Protocols laboratory manuals, and even the full text of select Wiley print books online.

What are some special features of Wiley InterScience?

Wiley Interscience Alerts is a service that delivers table of contents via e-mail for any journal available on Wiley InterScience as soon as a new issue is published online.
Early View is Wiley's exclusive service presenting individual articles online as soon as they are ready, even before the release of the compiled print issue. These articles are complete, peer-reviewed, and citable.
CrossRef is the innovative multi-publisher reference linking system enabling readers to move seamlessly from a reference in a journal article to the cited publication, typically located on a different server and published by a different publisher.

How can I access Wiley InterScience?

Visit http://www.interscience.wiley.com.

Guest Users can browse Wiley InterScience for unrestricted access to journal Tables of Contents and Article Abstracts, or use the powerful search engine.
Registered Users are provided with a *Personal Home Page* to store and manage customized alerts, searches, and links to favorite journals and articles. Additionally, Registered Users can view free Online Sample Issues and preview selected material from major reference works.
Licensed Customers are entitled to access full-text journal articles in PDF, with select journals also offering full-text HTML.

How do I become an Authorized User?

Authorized Users are individuals authorized by a paying Customer to have access to the journals in Wiley InterScience. For example, a University that subscribes to Wiley journals is considered to be the Customer. Faculty, staff and students authorized by the University to have access to those journals in Wiley InterScience are Authorized Users. Users should contact their Library for information on which Wiley journals they have access to in Wiley InterScience.